FIRST
IN PEACE

FIRST ❧ IN PEACE

George Washington, the Constitution, and the Presidency

JOHN ROSENBURG

The Millbrook Press
Brookfield, Connecticut

To Jean and Charles Chapin,
Robert B. Durham Jr., Augustus Hulit,
Robert Myers, and Amy and
Michael Ward. For the Memories.

JR

Photographs courtesy of The Mount Vernon Ladies' Association: pp. 8, 129; National Portrait Gallery/Smithsonian Institution/Art Resource, NY: pp. 18, 32, 60, 96, 187; Independence National Historic Park: p. 26; Library of Congress: p. 39; The Historical Society of Pennsylvania: pp. 47, 117, 246; North Wind Picture Archives: pp. 90, 165; Print Collection. Miriam and Ira D. Wallach Division of Art, Prints and Photographs. The New York Public Library. Astor, Lenox and Tilden Foundation: pp. 141 (Stokes #1789B-124), 216 (Stokes #1792-B-136); Brooklyn Museum of Art, Gift of the Crescent-Hamilton Athletic Club: p. 157 (#39.536.1); © Collection of The New-York Historical Society: p. 178; Collection of the Albany Institute of History and Art, Bequest of George Clinton Genet: p. 211; The Metropolitan Museum of Art: pp. 225 (Gift of Edgar, William and Bernice Chrysler Garbisch, 1963. 63.201.2), 235 (Bequest of Charles Allen Munn, 1924. 24.109.82)

Library of Congress Cataloging-in-Publication Data
Rosenburg, John M.
First in peace : George Washington, the Constitution, and the presidency / John Rosenburg.
p. cm.
Summary: A biography of the first president of the newly formed United States, George Washington, from his involvement in the Constitutional Convention in 1787, through his two terms as president, up to his death in 1799.
ISBN 0-7613-0422-3 (lib. bdg.)
1. Washington, George, 1732–1799–Juvenile literature. 2. Presidents–United States–Biography–Juvenile literature. 3. United States–Politics and government–1783–1809–Juvenile literature. [1. Washington, George, 1732–1799. 2. Presidents. 3. United States–Politics and government–1783–1809.] I. Title.
E312.R66 1998 973.4'1'092–dc21 [B] 98-18631 CIP AC

Published by The Millbrook Press, Inc.
2 Old New Milford Road
Brookfield, Connecticut 06804

FIRST
IN PEACE

Prologue

In the banquet hall in the North wing of Mount Vernon at about noon on April 14, 1789, an old friend and patriot, Charles Thomson, the Secretary of Congress, stood politely and respectfully before George Washington and delivered this brief but critically important message:

"Sir, as the President of the Senate chosen for the special occasion, having opened and counted the votes of the election in the presence of the Senate and House of Representatives, I was honored with the commands of the Senate to wait upon your Excellency with the information of your being elected to the office of the President of the United States."

George Washington learned that he had been unanimously elected the first president of the United States in the banquet hall at his home in Virginia, Mount Vernon.

At Washington's convenience, Thomson added, he would accompany the former commander in chief to New York, where the Senate and House of Representatives were waiting, "convened for the dispatch of public business."

Thomson then drew a letter from a small pouch he was carrying, adjusted his spectacles, and said softly, "I have here, your Excellency, the formal notification from the President of the Senate."

Satisfied he had the understanding and attention of the little audience before him, which included Martha Washington, her two grandchildren, Washington's secretary, Tobias Lear, and his wartime aide, David Humphreys, Thomson, with obvious satisfaction, raised his voice and read the "notification" aloud.

"Sir, I have the honor to transmit to your Excellency the information of your unanimous election to the Office of President of the United States of America. Suffer me, Sir, to indulge the hope that so auspicious a mark of public confidence will meet with your approbation, and be considered as a sure pledge of the affection and support you are to expect from a free and enlightened people.

"I am, sir, with Sentiments of Respect, your obedient humble servant, John Langdon."

For a moment or two, George Washington was silent and still, as were the others in that tastefully furnished, high-ceilinged room. It was as though all were digesting and weighing the portent of the words they had just heard.

Washington broke away from the group and walked to a window to stare out at the grounds of his beloved home, a home that he was just beginning to enjoy and hated to leave. Would

George Washington accept this unprecedented appointment?

For months, as the election returns staggered in from the thirteen states, he hesitated, ever mindful of the fact that his lengthy, historic call for a "Federal Convention" six years earlier was coupled with a firm pledge that he would never again take "any share in public business."

Publicly, as a result, he wouldn't say yes and he wouldn't say no to pleas that he accept the leading role in America's novel attempt at self-government. Washington did, however, let his friends know he faced a difficult choice, and why.

Only six months before Thomson's arrival at Mount Vernon, Washington told Benjamin Lincoln, one of his former generals, that if he were to accept the presidency, "I call Heaven to witness that this very act would be the greatest sacrifice of my personal feelings and wishes that ever I have been called upon to make. It would be to forgo the repose and domestic enjoyments for trouble, perhaps for public obloquy [abuse]; for I should consider myself entering upon an unexplored field, enveloped on every side with clouds and darkness."

But now, as his friends and family and the rest of the nation waited, he could no longer dodge the issue. Turning abruptly from the window, his large, graying head erect and his narrow shoulders back, Washington faced Thomson, then said in a deep, firm voice, "Since the opinion is unanimous, I hardly have an option."

After a pause, he went on, "Whatever my private feelings and sentiments may be, the only way to express my deep appreciation for the honor my countrymen have shown me is to accept the appointment. I will be ready to leave the day after tomorrow."

This decision, so simply expressed, so brief, clear, and direct, carried enormous implications; not only for the United States in the immediate and long-term future, but for the entire world.

It meant, after all, that for the very first time in the history of mankind the government of a country would be in the hands of the governed and not those of a king, emperor, or dictator.

This is the story of how this unique government, known as a democracy, was born, how it evolved, and how Washington helped give it life.

Book One

When George Washington galloped up to the door of Mount Vernon astride his favorite war horse, Old Nelson, on December 24, 1783, he was a happy man.

He had, after all, finally been able to keep a promise he had been forced to break many times: "I will be home by Christmas Eve," he had written from his headquarters that winter.

More important, the day before his arrival he had appeared before Congress in Annapolis, Maryland, and tendered his resignation as commander in chief of a victorious Continental Army, America's first.

In doing so, he left behind the most complicated, dangerous, distressful, and vexatious military and political assignment in United States history.

For almost nine years, without a single day of rest, Washington had led a fluctuating force of inexperienced, undertrained, underfed, undisciplined, underarmed, underpaid, and poorly clothed patriots against vastly superior numbers of British soldiers and German mercenaries with far better training.

Without doubt, America's enemy in the "war for independence" included the best trained, armed, provisioned and equipped troops in the world. And while the new nation was without a conventional navy, its opponent's army was supported by the biggest and best then in existence.

Washington also had to deal twice with traitors who tried to pass vital secrets to the British that surely would have had devastating consequences. Virtually every year, he was faced with the need to raise a new army. He was betrayed by several of his own generals, and he endured a plot which would force him to resign in disgrace.

In addition, Washington had to contend with politicians representing states that were uncooperative and jealous of each other. He also suffered a series of humiliating defeats, sometimes because his men refused to fight. Disease and desertions constantly depleted his troops.

And often, in the worst winter weather imaginable, he and his men were without adequate food, shelter, and clothing while his pleas for help were ignored by Congress and the state governments.

Several times, various units in the army mutinied. Twice he was forced to execute the ringleaders. And once, a group within his own command planned to assassinate him. Worse yet, in America's most dangerous hour, he faced down a mutiny by his officers that threatened to turn the nation into a military dictatorship.

Thus, it came as no surprise to those who knew him that he rejoiced in his new-found freedom, convinced that, at last, a long, peaceful life lay ahead of him, the mental and physical strain of public service left behind forever.

In a letter to his friend and former comrade-in-arms, the Marquis de Lafayette, Washington wrote, "At length, my dear Marquis, I am become a private citizen on the banks of the Potomac, and under the shadow of my own vine and my own fig tree."

"I am not only retired from all public employments," he added, "but I am retiring within myself, and shall be able to view the solitary walk and tread the paths of private life with heartfelt satisfaction. Envious of none, I am determined to be pleased with all, and this, my dear friend, being the order for my march, I will move gently down the stream of life until I sleep with my fathers."

But it was all a dream that was not to be.

During Washington's first few months at home, Mount Vernon was in the grip of extremely severe winter weather. In bitter cold, sheets of thick ice and several inches of snow covered the fields, buildings, and woods, clogged streams and ponds, and made roads impassable.

When weather conditions improved, a restless Washington plunged into the enormous task of managing his property, a tract of land that stretched some ten miles along the Potomac River and, at one point, was four miles wide.

While the main house and the land immediately adjacent to it were inherited from Washington's older half-brother, Lawrence, the rest had been purchased bit by bit and pieced together over many years. Much of this property was in woodland, but it contained five farms with hundreds of acres that were in pasture or under cultivation.

The farms were stocked with sheep, cattle, horses, oxen, fowl, and enough hogs to provide nearly eight tons of pork a year. Part of the property resembled a small village with numerous buildings, including farmhouses, slave cabins, barns, a schoolhouse, and shops for brewers, carpenters, and a blacksmith. Washington also owned and operated a busy gristmill and a ferry used to carry the public back and forth across the Potomac.

Beginning at dawn, his days were full. And not only because he devoted almost all of his daylight hours to the demanding routine of farming, but because he had suddenly become something America had never known before: a national hero.

Everyone, it seemed, wanted to see him, talk to him, and, if possible, shake his hand. Wherever he went, near or far, a committee instantly sprang into existence to honor and applaud him. Often, there were parades followed by thirteen-gun salutes—one for each state—and speeches punctuated with thirteen toasts.

Even when he visited his elderly mother, Mary Ball Washington, in Fredricksburg on February 12, he was welcomed with a formal address. Naturally, he gave a polite response. There was also a dinner in his honor the next day—with more speeches and more toasts.

Not surprisingly, scores of people called at his home, including a long list of distinguished foreigners. Many who arrived at his door came without invitations. And some were impostors.

But since Mount Vernon was a long way from a town or tavern, Washington's visitors often stayed for a meal, or overnight. On one occasion, fifteen travelers joined the family. As for George and Martha, they were not able to dine alone until June 30, 1785, eighteen months after he returned from the war.

Through it all, Washington was gracious and hospitable. And he rarely changed a routine that kept him at his "chores" and had him in bed by nine o'clock.

By the spring of 1784, Washington's thinking had changed about many matters, but physically, the fifty-two-year-old Washington was pretty much the same as when he had reluctantly accepted command of the ragged Patriot troops that kept a large contingent of the British Army under siege in Boston nine years earlier.

Taller than the average American of his day by some six to nine inches, he still carried his powerful six-foot-three-inch frame with the steady, lithe, and graceful tread of an athlete. His shoulders and his large head were always erect, whether sitting his horse or standing. His stomach was flat and hard, his big hands and long arms as strong as ever.

Washington's reddish-brown hair was turning gray, of course. And his blue-gray eyes had weakened somewhat, forcing him to use eyeglasses to read. He also had a touch of rheuma-

This family portrait, done in the 1790s, shows the Washingtons along with Martha's two grandchildren, Eleanor "Nelly" Custis and George Washington Parke Custis, who was sometimes known as "Little Washington."

tism in his left arm and shoulder, and his dental plate—with human teeth screwed crudely into it—bothered him because it didn't fit his gums properly.

While he worked hard to enhance the beauty of the manor house and the land around it, his greatest source of pleasure and comfort was his family. His twenty-five year marriage to Martha, who was also fifty-two, was stronger than ever. While they had never had children, Martha's grandchildren, four-year-old Eleanor "Nelly" Custis and three-year-old George Washington Parke Custis (called "Tub" by some and "Little Washington" by others), were a constant joy. Soon, however, Washington's busy, cherished life began to crumble.

"An indissoluble Union of the State under one Federal Head."

That was the gist of Washington's plea to Congress and the states in 1783 after the war ended. In what would become known as "Washington's Legacy," he said, "It is yet to be decided whether the Revolution must ultimately be considered as a blessing or a curse; a blessing or a curse, not in the present age alone, for with our fate will the destiny of unborn millions be involved."

Now, three years later, it appeared that while the war was won, the peace was very far from secure. And the country's destiny remained in question.

Every day for months, the news brought to Washington by visitors, and that contained in the constant flow of letters and "gazettes" (newspapers) he received, made it clear that a wide range of growing problems seriously threatened the new nation that had already paid a terrible price to achieve freedom and independence for its people. The problems included:

• A huge debt with no source of income.

• Internal disorders.

• Threats from external forces (England, in defiance of the peace treaty put in place after the war, still occupied forts on the western frontier. Spain occupied New Orleans and parts of Florida).

• Lack of a unified domestic and international trade policy.

• Lack of an immigration policy.

• Lack of plans for westward expansion.

• Lack of a uniform monetary policy.

• Thirteen state governments that acted independently and fought among themselves over many issues, such as fishing rights and interstate commerce.

• Lack of an adequate defense. (The Continental Army had been reduced to 672 officers and men; a navy didn't exist.)

Washington blamed this deplorable state of affairs on a single document: the Articles of Confederation. "It's weak, it's flawed, it's practically useless," Washington once said.

The Articles of Confederation, adopted by Congress in 1777 and ratified by the states in

1781, held the Union together and, while it was in effect, defined the nation. Under its terms, Congress was a single body with a rotating president who had virtually no power other than to run meetings and appoint committees.

"Each State retains its sovereignty, freedom, and independence," the Articles declared. It also gave each state one vote regardless of its size or circumstances. Repeatedly, Washington asked, "How can thirteen independent states—each of a different size and with different economic and social interests—successfully share in operating a national government?"

Often, as Martha sat with him in the library sewing and knitting while he read his mail and the gazettes, he would explode with indignation at something negative he had just read. Early in 1786, however, his hopes for a stable government soared.

"Martha!" he fairly shouted as he waved a copy of the *Virginia Gazette* in her direction. "Listen!" He read aloud a resolution passed by Virginia's general assembly: "Resolved that Edmund Randolph, James Madison, Walter Jones, St. George Tucker, and Meriwether Smith be appointed commissioners who shall meet such commissioners as may be appointed by the other states in the Union to take into consideration the trade of the United States; to examine the relative situations and trade of the said states; to consider how far a uniform system in their commercial regulations may be necessary to their common interest and their permanent harmony; and to report to the several states, such an act relative to this great object as, when unanimously ratified by them, will enable the United States in Congress effectually to provide for same."

Martha was puzzled. "But what does it mean, that last line?" she asked.

"It means that maybe—just maybe—the states are going to try to work together!" he answered.

"It doesn't sound very promising to me," she said.

"Maybe not," Washington responded. "But it's a step—a small step, I'll admit—but it's in the right direction."

Little did Washington—or anyone else—realize how far that small step would take America. Or how it would affect Washington's life.

Virginia's call prompted the states to schedule a convention in Annapolis, Maryland, for September 1786. Washington was elated.

In a letter to a friend written in August that year, he wrote: "The greater part of the Union seems to be convinced of the necessity of federal measures, and of investing Congress with the power of regulating the commerce of the whole."

On September 9, he wrote to a neighbor, Colonel John Fitzgerald, and asked, "Have you heard from Annapolis since Monday? Have the commercial commissioners met? Have they proceeded to business? How long is it supposed their sessions will last? And is it likely they will do anything effectual?"

He found answers to all his questions in letters from the Virginia delegates and in newspapers. Washington's reaction was decidedly mixed. He was, for example, angry and disappointed to learn that only five of the thirteen states were represented!

On the other hand, he was pleased to discover that the fourteen delegates who did attend the Annapolis convention unanimously adopted a bold and startling proposal, written by Alexander Hamilton, calling for all the states to send delegates to another convention in Philadelphia to be held on the second Monday in May, 1787. The purpose? As Hamilton said: "To take into consideration the situation of the United States, to devise such provisions as shall appear to them necessary to render the constitution of the federal government adequate to the exigencies of the Union; and to report such an act for that purpose to the United States in Congress assembled, as, when agreed to by them, and afterwards confirmed by the legislatures of every state, will effectually provide for the same."

A constitution "adequate to the exigencies of the Union?" Surely that meant strengthening the Articles of Confederation. Finally, Washington exulted, the country was going to try to right itself. It would become the true "union" he had long dreamed of.

But wait! Would the delegates to Congress agree to a federal convention? They, after all, were sent to Congress by the states. Since only five states voted on Hamilton's proposal, would Congress take his resolution seriously?

And should Congress summon delegates to Philadelphia, would the convention—in terms of attendance—fare any better than the one just held in Annapolis?

For days, Congress was silent on the subject and the so-called "united" states continued to drift.

Then, without warning, a disaster was in the making—serious disturbances had erupted in New England.

David Humphreys, Washington's former aide-de-camp, sent word that mobs had threatened courts and judges in various parts of New England and everything was "in a state of confusion."

Writing from his home in Hartford, Connecticut, in the fall of 1786, Humphreys added, "I have just now seen accounts of tumults in New Hampshire. General Sullivan has behaved nobly and put a period to a very considerable insurrection without effusion of blood. Rhode Island continues in a state of frenzy and division on account of their paper currency."

Alarmed, Washington promptly wrote Humphreys asking, "For God's sake, tell me what is the cause of all these commotions? Do they proceed from licentiousness, British influence disseminated by the Tories, or real grievances which admit of redress? If the latter, why were they delayed till the popular mind had become so agitated? If the former, why are not the powers of Government tried at once?"

As Washington sought answers to these questions, the reports of disorders continued to pour into Mount Vernon. The most alarming came from Henry Knox, a former general who was now secretary of war. The insurrec-

David Humphreys was Washington's aide-de-camp in the Continental Army and a lifelong friend.

tionists, Knox said, believed that the "property of the United States has been protected from Britain by the joint exertions of all, and therefore ought to be the common property of all. And he that attempts opposition to this creed is an enemy to equity and justice and ought to be swept off the face of the earth."

Knox added that some twelve to fifteen thousand "desperate and unprincipled" troublemakers were "determined to annihilate all debts public and private."

When Washington showed the letter from their old friend to Martha, her roundish, attractive features and blue eyes clouded with concern. Putting the letter down, she said, "Twelve to fifteen thousand?"

"Yes," Washington said. "And if they come together, that would be a bigger army than I had during most of the Revolution."

Martha was horrified. "Why, George," she said, "this could lead to anarchy!" Washington nodded in grim agreement.

The basic problem fueling the disorders in New England was paper money that could not be backed by "hard" currency (such as gold or silver), money made virtually worthless by inflation.

As Washington explained to Martha in the privacy of the library before dinner one evening, the value of paper money depreciated rapidly everywhere in the country because of the war.

"Those who borrowed before and during the war can't find enough of today's inflated dollars to pay their debts," he said. "And I'm no exception."

"What does that mean?" Martha asked in sudden alarm.

"It means that those who borrowed from me can't pay me. And that I can't pay those from whom I borrowed."

"George!"

"It's true. But, for now, I'm not pressing my debtors and my creditors are not pressing me."

In some states, he went on to explain, those in debt got help from the state government and were able to stave off foreclosure on the property they owned. Not so in Massachusetts. As a result, the farmers—the hardest-hit group—often got together and stormed courthouses to keep judges from ordering foreclosure on their farms and throwing the debtors among them in jail.

"Unless a solution is found, these disorders will spread and could prove disastrous," Washington said with a sad shake of his head. Just about then, Washington heard from Congressman "Light Horse Harry" Lee, who suggested that Washington pay a visit to New York and New England to use his "influence" to end the disorders.

"Good God!" Washington replied. "Who besides a Tory could have foreseen, or a Briton predicted these disorders? I am mortified beyond expression when I view the clouds that have spread over the brightest morn that ever dawned upon any country.

"What a triumph for our enemies, to verify their predictions! What a triumph for advocates of despotism, to find that we are incapable of governing ourselves, and that systems founded on the basis of equal liberty, are merely ideal and fallacious."

He added that he knew "not where" the influence Lee alluded to could be found and "if attainable, that it would be a proper remedy for the disorders."

And then he noted sternly: "Influence is no government."

Early in November 1786, Washington heard from David Humphreys again.

"The troubles in Massachusetts still continue," Humphreys said. "Government is prostrated in the dust. And it is much to be feared that there is not energy enough in that state to reestablish the civil powers. The leaders of the mob, whose fortune and measures are desperate, are strengthening themselves daily; and it is expected they will soon take possession of the continental arsenal at Springfield, in which there are from ten to fifteen thousand stands of arms in excellent order.

"Congress, I am told, are seriously alarmed and hardly know which way to turn, or what to expect. Indeed, my dear General, nothing but a good Providence can extricate us from the present difficulties and prevent some terrible catastrophe."

Then came two lines that caused Washington's heart to sink:

"In case of civil discord, I have already told you it was seriously my opinion that you could not remain neutral, and that you would be obliged, in self defense, to take part on one side or the other, or withdraw from the continent. Your friends are of the same opinion."

Take one side or the other? Leave Mount Vernon? The continent? Were these the only choices for Washington?

No! The Philadelphia convention offered the solution. Get the states together to strengthen the central government before it was too late!

"Virginia is the largest state," Washington told Martha as he paced fretfully about the library. "It should lead the way." After a brief silence he added, "I'll write Richmond tomorrow."

Although concerned about his involvement, Martha asked only one question. "To whom are you going to write?"

"Jemmy," he said.

"No bigger than half a piece of soap."

That's the way someone once described 36-year-old James "Jemmy" Madison.

Although slight of build with a soft, low voice, Madison was, intellectually, a giant. Even though he was almost twenty years younger than Washington, they were close friends and corresponded frequently about a subject that was of great concern to both: the survival of the United States.

In writing to Madison in November 1786, Washington included the reports from Knox and Humphreys.

"What stronger evidence can be given of the want of energy in our governments than these disorders?" Washington asked. "If there exists not a power to check them, what security has a man for life, liberty, or property?"

Although he was several years younger than Washington, James Madison was one of the president's trusted confidants and advisers.

Then he added: "Thirteen sovereignties pulling against each other and all tugging at the federal head will soon bring ruin to the whole, whereas a liberal and energetic constitution, well guarded and closely watched to prevent encroachments, might restore us to that degree of respectability and consequence to which we had a fair claim and the brightest prospect of attaining."

Virginia, he told Madison, should be among the first to respond to the call for the Philadelphia convention. But Madison, a member of the Virginia legislature, had apparently already pushed for such a move.

"It has been thought advisable to give this subject a very solemn dress and all the weight that could be derived from a single state," Madison responded. A delegation had been selected, he said. And Washington had been named to lead it.

Knowing how much Washington cherished his life with Martha at Mount Vernon, Madison added, "It is not necessary, however, to make an immediate decision."

Two months later, Washington's worst fears were realized. The angry, disorganized farmers in Massachusetts, he learned, had rallied behind a leader. His name was Daniel Shays.

Following the Revolution, the money-starved states dealt with poverty and indebtedness in different ways. Rhode Island, for example, allowed debtors to use script—paper that was worthless—to pay taxes and debts. If a creditor refused to accept the script, the debtor had only to deposit it with the nearest judge and his debt would be wiped out.

While other states used other schemes, Massachusetts tried to establish a sound fiscal policy based on the adage "a bargain is a bargain and must be made good." In other words, taxes and other debts had to be paid in full with hard currency. But hard currency was so scarce it was almost nonexistent, especially in farming areas.

The lack of money created this dilemma: To pay for goods they had imported, seaport merchants pressed storekeepers to pay for merchandise ordered and delivered. Storekeepers then pressed farmers and others for goods purchased so they could pay the importers.

Those who couldn't pay—usually farmers—were taken to court and, in most cases, stripped of their land, livestock, and belongings and jailed. In Worcester County alone, ninety-two people were imprisoned in 1785.

The western area farmers retaliated by storming courthouses to prevent judges from hearing cases against debtors. For the most part, the protests were disorganized and ineffectual. When Daniel Shays became the leader of the movement, however, matters suddenly became serious.

Shays had fought in the Revolution as a captain in the Massachusetts militia, serving gallantly at Bunker Hill. He was an honest, hard-working but poor man, so poor that he had to sell a sword presented to him by Lafayette so he could pay a debt.

In late January 1787, Shays led twelve hundred men armed with pitchforks, barrel staves, shovels, and a few guns to Springfield with two objectives: to seize the Federal arsenal and distribute the arms it contained to his men; and to prevent the Supreme Court from sitting so the judges could not indict the farmers for treason.

Acting swiftly, Massachusetts authorities rushed Major General William Sheperd to the arsenal with several hundred militia from the eastern counties. When Shays and his followers marched toward the arsenal, Sheperd's troops opened up with artillery, forcing Shays's men to scatter.

Early in February, Benjamin Lincoln, a Revolutionary War general, arrived on the scene during a snowstorm with more militia. Although Shays escaped to Vermont, Lincoln's troops quickly pursued and captured several of his men. In a few hours, Shays's Rebellion was over. But the impact of that brief struggle was not. "The Tories are laughing at us," Washington wrote to a friend. "They said all along we couldn't govern ourselves. Now, they are convinced of it."

Once Shays's Rebellion had made it clear that the central government could be of no help to the states in a crisis, public opinion changed and the proposed Philadelphia convention seemed as if it could be a success. While Washington had been named a member of the Virginia delegation along with Governor Edmund Randolph, James Madison, and George Mason, many wondered: Would he attend?

Washington's letters to friends showed he had deep reservations about going to the convention.

"Suppose the states refuse to send delegates to the convention and it fails?" he asked. "If I attend, will not this lack of interest reflect on my reputation?

"And if I don't attend, will that indicate I have no faith in our country? In my convictions? Or will the public believe I do not think attendance is worth the effort?

"And what of my pledge to never again intermeddle in public affairs? What will the public think if I now suddenly reverse myself? Will they not think I am for personal gain of some sort?"

He noted that four of Virginia's most important men—Thomas Jefferson, Patrick Henry, Thomas Nelson Jr., and Richard Henry Lee—

had, for various reasons, turned down invitations to attend the convention.

"Who will attend from the other states?" he asked. "Will they be men of ability and knowledge? Or will they be men who are more concerned with personal interests than those of our country?"

Washington was also concerned about his health and his finances, neither of which, he felt, would allow him to stay in Philadelphia for any great length of time.

As the second Monday in May, the fourteenth, came closer, however, Washington made up his mind: He would go, but with misgivings.

"I very much fear," he told Governor Randolph, "that all the States will not appear in convention, and that some of them will come fettered so as to impede rather than accelerate the great object of their convening, which, under the peculiar circumstances of my case, would place me in a more disagreeable situation than any other member."

While Washington's decision was widely applauded, it was clear that the new nation would be confronted with a critical question: With some four million people spread thinly across thirteen states steeped in different customs, manners, and circumstances, what, if anything, could be accomplished by revising the Articles of Confederation?

Although the war had ended almost four years earlier, America had not forgotten the accomplishments of the former commander in chief of its Continental Army.

Arriving at the outskirts of Philadelphia on the 13th of May, Washington was greeted by the City Light Horse and scores of mounted civilians. As he entered the city of some forty thousand inhabitants, several cannons boomed a hearty welcome and church bells rang continuously. And despite a heavy rain, huge crowds gathered along the route waving flags, applauding, and cheering wildly.

Washington had planned to stay at a "genteel" boardinghouse at Fifth and Market streets, but financier Robert Morris and his wife insisted he stay with them in what was regarded as the finest home in Philadelphia, the very house his opponent, Sir William Howe, commander of the British forces, had occupied during the Revolution.

Before settling in that day, however, Washington called on Benjamin Franklin, the president of Pennsylvania and Philadelphia's most prestigious resident. He had not seen the former ambassador to France and England since they both attended the Second Continental Congress in 1776. As might be expected, the exchange of greetings was warm and effusive.

The Constitutional Convention took place at Independence Hall in Philadelphia. Before the new nation declared its independence on July 4, 1776, the building had been known as the State House.

The Convention was to start the next morning at 10 o'clock in the handsome, high-ceilinged, forty-by-forty-foot East Room of the State House, now called Independence Hall.

On two sides of the room, high, wide windows let in an abundance of light unless the slotted blinds were closed, which they often were in summer to keep out the sun.

A high-backed chair for the presiding officer was in place in the middle of the east wall with a covered table in front of it. And in front of the table, a low bar with a gate in the middle stretched across the room from north to south.

In the main body of the room, comfortable chairs were set up at tables covered in green fabric to accommodate the delegates.

Punctual as always, Washington was the first member of the Virginia delegation to arrive in the East Room. Entering with a brisk stride, he moved quickly to a desk and took a seat.

But the only delegates to arrive that day were from Virginia and Pennsylvania. Among the latter was the ailing eighty-one-year-old Franklin, who entered the Hall in an elaborate sedan chair he had brought with him from France. (The chair, partly enclosed in glass, was carried by four convicts "borrowed" from the city jail.)

"This is not a very good start," Washington grumbled to his fellow delegates.

Madison tried to soothe Washington's ruffled feathers. "I think we can attribute the delay to bad roads and poor weather," he said.

It was true, of course, that extremely wet weather had turned many roads to mud and made traveling exceedingly difficult. And since most of the delegates were traveling over long distances on horseback (two Georgia delegates would cover eight hundred miles), a delay was understandable.

Early each day, the Virginia and Pennsylvania delegations went to the meeting hall to learn whether the Convention was able to muster the necessary quorum (majority) of seven states.

They were disappointed on the 15th and 16th. On the 17th, South Carolina appeared. A day later, the New York delegation trudged into the hall. And three days later, on the 18th, Delaware's contingent arrived. After another four days passed, North Carolina showed up.

Still, one more fully qualified state was needed before the Convention could proceed. When none reported on the 23rd, or 24th, a discouraged Washington wondered aloud, "Is this going to be another 'Annapolis'?"

On the 25th, however, William Churchill Houston of New Jersey, although severely weakened by illness, walked through the door at exactly 10 o'clock.

In doing so, Churchill filled out the slate of three from his state, giving the Convention a quorum of four states from the South and three states from the North. In all, there were now twenty-nine delegates on hand.

Eleven days after its scheduled start, the Convention opened by addressing what was obviously the first order of business: The selection of the presiding officer.

For a handful of delegates in the chamber that day, it was an eerie moment. Once before—in the same room, but then as members of the Second Continental Congress—they and their country faced a different crisis: war with England.

Then, as now, they were asked to choose a man to lead their little nation to safety. On the earlier occasion, John Adams, a delegate from Massachusetts, recommended a "gentleman from Virginia" for the post of commander in chief.

Realizing that Adams was about to nominate him, an embarrassed Washington had left his seat and disappeared into the library a few steps away.

When rumors began to surface that he might be elected, Washington said repeatedly that he was unqualified for such an important command and tried to avoid it. On June 15, 1775, however, he was elected unanimously.

Now, nearly twelve years later, history seemed ready to repeat itself. On May 25, 1787, Robert Morris, Washington's host and a Pennsylvania delegate, rose to say, "Gentlemen, on behalf of Mr. Franklin, who is not well today, and on instructions from the elected representatives of Pennsylvania, I have the honor to nominate General George Washington as president of this Convention."

Morris was barely back in his seat before John Rutledge of South Carolina stood and, in ringing tones, said, "I second the motion."

Rutledge, an authoritative man known as "Dictator John," cast a meaningful look about the chamber and added, "And I hope, gentlemen, the vote will be unanimous." It was.

This time, Washington did not leave the room, making it clear that he was committed to the fashioning of a new and stronger central government.

At the conclusion of the vote, which was swiftly completed, Robert Morris and John Rutledge escorted Washington to the chair.

When they left him, Washington looked solemnly around the great hall and said, "Gentlemen, I thank you for the honor you have bestowed on me. Since I am now to act in a role totally foreign to me and to which I am hardly qualified, I trust you will forgive my mistakes, of which, I am sure there will be many." His remarks were greeted with good-natured laughter and a warm round of applause.

That same day—a Saturday—the delegates got down to business and elected a doorkeeper, a secretary to keep a daily journal, a messenger, and, most important, a rules committee. By then, it was time to adjourn. "Ten o'clock Monday," Washington said with a bang of his gavel.

By Monday, several more delegates had arrived. On the same day, the rules committee, chaired by George Wythe of Virginia, was ready to address the Convention. The sixty-year-old Wythe, a signer of the Declaration of Independence and a lawyer and jurist, was a sharp-featured man with a long nose and chin.

The proposed rules Wythe read to his fellow delegates were simple and direct. "Every member rising to speak, shall address the president; and whilst he shall be speaking, none shall pass between them, or hold discourse with another, or read a book, pamphlet or paper, printed or manuscript," Wythe read. "A member shall not speak oftener than twice, without special leave, upon the same question and not the second time, before every other, who had been silent, shall have been heard, if he chooses to speak upon the subject.

"When the house shall adjourn," he added, "every member shall stand in his place until the president pass him."

There were other important rules:

• Seven states were to be a quorum.

• If a quorum was established, a majority of the fully represented states could decide all questions.

• Matters passed on by the majority could be reconsidered by the House "when they see cause."

• The house could, at any time, form a "committee of the whole," a device that allowed the president to leave his chair and join the rest of the delegates in discussing any important issue. And when the session resorted to a "committee of the whole," votes and positions could be changed. In effect, it gave the delegates a free-wheeling opportunity to air all sides of an issue without being held to an earlier position or vote.

One rule, however, was virtually unheard of: secrecy. Under this rule, "nothing spoken in the house" was to be printed "or otherwise published, or communicated to anyone not directly involved in the Convention without permission . . . for the duration of the Convention."

There were several reasons for this rule. Primarily, the delegates feared that "leaks" could spark debates outside the Convention and jeopardize the proceedings. All wanted to be able to speak freely and change positions during the course of the meetings.

"All in favor say 'aye.'" Washington called out when the rules were ready to be put to a vote.

"Aye," the house roared back.

"All opposed, say 'nay.'" Washington said. There was no response.

The next day—Tuesday, May 29—most of the delegates, as they had been instructed, were ready to discuss revising the Articles of Confederation and believed that they were about to do so.

They were shocked to learn differently.

For the eleven days the Convention was without a quorum, Washington and the rest of the Virginia delegates had been far from idle.

Meeting day after day in taverns with names like Indian Queen, City Tavern, George, or Black Horse, the delegation had arrived at a critically important and unexpected decision so innovative and bold it would, when unveiled,

In a four-hour presentation, Governor Edmund Randolph unveiled the Virginia Plan, which established the framework of a new form of government for the United States.

stun the Convention. And, eventually, the rest of the nation.

When Washington called the meeting to order on the morning of the 29th, the day after the rules were adopted, Edmund Randolph, Virginia's thirty-two-year-old governor, sprang to his feet. Standing tall and straight after being recognized by the chair, he gave a presentation that took almost four hours. This is the way he began:

"To prevent the fulfillment of the prophecies of the downfall of the United States, it is our duty to inquire into the defects of the [Articles of] Confederation and the requisite properties of the government now to be framed; the danger of the situation and its remedy.

"The Confederation was made in the infancy of the science of constitutions, when the inefficiency of requisitions was unknown; when no commercial discord had arisen among states; when no rebellion like that in Massachusetts had broken out; when foreign debts were not urgent; when the havoc of paper money had not been foreseen; when treaties had not been violated; and when nothing better could have been conceded by states jealous of their sovereignty.

"But it offered no security against foreign invasions, for Congress could neither prevent nor conduct a war, nor punish infractions of treaties or of the law of nations, nor control particular states from provoking war.

"The federal government has no constitutional power to check a quarrel between separate states; nor to suppress a rebellion in any one of them; nor to establish a productive impost [tax]; nor to counteract the commercial regulations of other nations; nor to defend itself against encroachments of the states.

"From the manner in which it has been ratified in many of the states, [the Articles of Confederation] cannot be claimed to be paramount to the state constitutions; so that there is a prospect of anarchy from the inherent laxity of government."

Pausing for a moment, Randolph looked around the room, then said solemnly, "As the remedy, the government to be established must have for its basis the republican principle."

The delegates shifted in their seats and exchanged looks. "The republican principle?" What did that mean? They would soon find out.

Having spelled out the weaknesses in the Articles of Confederation, Edmund Randolph now tried to soften the way for the plan hammered out by the Virginia delegation during the long hours before the Convention opened.

The Articles of Confederation, he said, were no stronger than any of the state constitutions, implying that they could not be used to govern the states or the nation.

"Look at the public countenance from New Hampshire to Georgia!" he cried. "Are we not on the eve of war, which is only prevented by the hopes from this Convention?"

He then introduced fifteen resolves developed by the Virginians. By the end of the day, the bare bones of a constitution were on the table for all the delegates to chew on.

These three proposals, however, would get the most attention:

• A "national legislature" that should "consist of two branches, of which the members of the first or democratic house ought to be elected by the people of the several states; of the second, by those of the first, out of persons nominated by the individual [state] legislatures."

• "A national executive, chosen by the national legislature and ineligible a second time."

• "A national judiciary . . . to consist of supreme and inferior tribunals; to be chosen by the national legislature."

In short, the backbone of the proposed government was to consist of three branches: legislative, executive, and judicial.

But as the delegates digested the overall plan, they made a startling discovery. Every member of the proposed three branches would—directly or indirectly—be elected by the inhabitants of the thirteen states. This meant a majority of qualified citizens could control their government if they would do but one simple thing: vote! It was a concept the world had never known.

Since he was president of the Convention, Washington rarely, if ever, commented on subjects that would come up while he was in the chair. He did, however, vote on many resolutions. And, like all of the delegates, he was free to change his vote while in committee of the whole.

Washington was not an impulsive voter or speaker. His military career had taught him to weigh matters carefully before he made a decision or comment. In war, after all, errors in judgment often led to loss of life or defeat.

"I like to put the sides of an argument on a scale," he once said. "If one side outweighs the other, that is the way I usually go."

On the day after the "Virginia plan" was introduced by Edmund Randolph, Washington turned the chair over to Nathaniel Gorham of Massachusetts so he could sit in committee.

Realizing that the country was in danger, the delegates of the nine states now represented lost no time in getting at the proposal laid before the convention by Randolph. Quickly approved was Resolve Number One, which declared that government should look to the nation's "common defense, security of liberty, and general welfare."

Resolve Number Two dealt with that most volatile of issues, the "sovereignty" of states. It was set aside temporarily so discussion could proceed on other matters, a tactic the delegates used repeatedly when obstacles to agreement were encountered.

Next, agreed to without dissent or debate, was the proposal concerning the "two branches" of the legislature. Only Benjamin Franklin and the Pennsylvania delegation favored a single chamber. (Pennsylvania later changed its vote.)

But now came the clause in Virginia's Resolve Number Four that read: "that the members of the first branch of the National Legislature ought to be elected by the people of the several States."

George Read of Delaware warned that his delegation had been instructed not to accept such a clause. If it was forced on them, he said, "it might become our duty to retire from the convention." Read's concern was that the more populous states could dominate his and other small states.

Roger Sherman of Connecticut and Elbridge Gerry of Massachusetts also objected to the clause. The sixty-six-year-old Sherman, tall, lean, and long-haired, was one of the most frequent speakers at the convention. Like Sherman, Gerry was also quite vocal. Physically, however, he was much different, being short and thin.

"The people should have nothing to do with government!" Sherman and Gerry insisted.

George Mason of Virginia disagreed. "The first branch will be the grand depository of the democratic principles of government!" he cried. "It is our House of Commons. It ought to know and sympathize with every part of the community, and it ought to be taken from different parts of the whole republic."

He said the government should protect the rights and happiness of both the "lowest and highest orders of citizens."

James Wilson of Pennsylvania vigorously supported Mason. "No government can long subsist without the confidence of its people," Wilson said.

James Madison then added his considerable weight to the argument. "The popular election of one branch of the national legislature is essential to every plan of free government," he said. "The great fabric to be raised by this Convention will be more stable and durable if it rests on the solid foundation of the people themselves."

Gerry and Sherman continued to object. So did Irish-born Pierce Butler of South Carolina, who said, "election by the people is impractical." The proposal, however, was adopted.

The delegates to the Convention were a remarkable lot.

In comparison to those who attended the Continental Congress, they were relatively young; the average age was forty-four, with four delegates under the age of thirty.

They were also intelligent, well-educated, experienced, and knowledgeable about government. Of the fifty-five delegates who eventually attended the Convention, nine had graduated from Princeton, four from Yale, three from Harvard, two from Columbia, three from the University of Pennsylvania, three from The Temple (a British law school), seven from the College of William and Mary, one from Oxford (England), and another had been educated at three universities in Scotland.

While Washington was the only delegate without a formal education of any kind, he had vast experience in government and politics, having served in the Virginia legislature for seventeen years and in both Continental Congresses. As commander in chief of the Continental Army during the American Revolution, he was constantly in contact with Congress and the various state governments.

Seven of Washington's fellow delegates had also been in the Continental Congress, and four had been on his staff during the Revolution. Thirteen others had been officers in the Continental Army and thirteen in militia units. Almost half of the delegates were lawyers or judges, and nearly all had held political posts in state government or on state committees. Before attending the Convention, many of the delegates, including Washington, had studied the makeup of governments in both ancient and modern times.

Obviously, the delegates to the Convention were well suited and equipped for the challenging and unprecedented task they faced. Still, the Convention bogged down almost immediately over the thorniest issue of all—sovereignty.

It was a word favored by several delegates because it meant supreme power, especially over a body politic; freedom from external control; autonomy; and controlling influence.

"Resolved that the Articles of Confederation ought to be so revised, corrected, and enlarged as to render the Federal Constitution adequate to the exigencies of Government and the preservation of the Union."

This statement began a new plan of government favored by the small states and introduced on June 9 by William Paterson of New Jersey, a keen-eyed man.

Under this plan, Congress would continue to be the single and main branch of government. More important, its members would not be elected by the people, but by the states they represented.

Since the Articles gave each state a single vote, size didn't matter. In other words, Delaware, with a population of less than 60,000, had the same power in Congress as Virginia, with 750,000 residents.

Small states, like Delaware, Connecticut, and New Jersey, were determined to keep their voting clout in the new national government.

"New Jersey will never confederate on the plan before the committee," Paterson said in an impassioned speech. "She would be swallowed up. I would rather submit to a monarch, to a despot than to such a fate. I will not only oppose the plan here, but on my return home do everything in my power to defeat it there."

James Wilson of Pennsylvania challenged Paterson immediately. Wilson, a smallish man with full cheeks and calm eyes, was the strongest supporter of the view that all power should rest in the people.

"Are not the citizens of Pennsylvania equal to those of New Jersey?" he barked. "Does it require one hundred and fifty of the former to balance fifty of the latter? If the small states will not confederate on this plan, Pennsylvania and, I presume, some other states, would not confederate on any other!"

Strangely enough, the "Paterson plan," as it was called, also won the support of Robert Yates and John Lansing Jr., two of the three delegates from the large state of New York.

"The New Jersey system," Lansing said, "is federal; the Virginia system national. In the first, the powers flow from the state governments; in the second they derive authority from the people of the states, and must ultimately annihilate the state governments."

Put another way, he said, the states would keep their sovereignty under the Paterson plan, but lose it under the Virginia plan.

The delegates, Lansing insisted, did not have the authority to do away with the Articles of

Confederation; they could only change them. And then he added bluntly: "If New York suspected an attempt would be made to form a national government, it would not have sent its delegates to Philadelphia."

With tempers rising and delegates of three states hinting that they might go home, the debate dragged on through the day. Early the next day, Saturday, supporters of the Paterson plan drew fire from Edmund Randolph. "When the salvation of the republic is at stake," he cried, "it would be treason to our trust not to propose what we find necessary.

"A national government, properly constituted, will alone answer the purpose. And this is the only moment when it can be established!

"View our present deplorable situation," he added with considerable emotion. "France, to whom we are indebted in every motive of gratitude and honor, is left unpaid by the large sums she supplied us with in the day of our necessity. Our officers and soldiers, who have successfully fought our battles, and the loaners of money to the public look up to you for relief. The bravery of our troops is degraded by the weakness of our government."

Randolph's argument lasted until noon, when the Convention adjourned. On Monday, yet another plan was put before the convention by New York's third delegate, Alexander Hamilton.

Thirty-two-year-old Alexander Hamilton was a brilliant, complex man called "The Little Lion" because of his boldness and courage. And while he and Washington were good friends, they didn't always agree. Hamilton and his fellow delegates from New York—Yates and Lansing—didn't agree, either. Not once, in fact, did they vote with him during the Convention.

For six hours—from the opening gavel to adjournment—Hamilton discussed his proposal.

"I have grave doubts," he commented, "whether a national government on the Virginia Plan can be effectual. The Virginia Plan is but pork still, with a little change of the sauce.

"The general government must not only have a strong soul, but strong organs by which that soul is to operate. The best form of government, not attainable by us, but the model to which we should approach as near as possible, is the British constitution," he added.

His plan called for:

• A single executive chosen for life with the power to veto—that is, cancel—any legislation put before him.

• The first chamber to be elected by the people for a term of three years.

• Senators to be elected, by electors, for life.

Alexander Hamilton advocated the adoption of a plan patterned after the British Constitution. Not surprisingly, this was not a popular idea.

• Governors of the states to be appointed by the national government.

His plan for the government, he said, "constitutes an elective monarchy; but by making the executive subject to impeachment the term monarchy cannot apply."

He went on to say that his plan would balance the power of the various branches of government. "Men love power," he explained. "Give all power to the many, they will oppress the few. Give all power to the few, they will oppress the many."

But the British form of government had at its head a king. The delegates knew that America had had enough of kings. And so they listened in polite silence throughout the day, even though in committee of the whole, they took no action on Hamilton's radical ideas and recommendations.

Nor would they ever forget that Alexander Hamilton favored the British form of government—a monarchy.

In the days that followed, the delegates continued to grapple in committee of the whole with this question: If there were to be two main branches of the legislature, how were the members to be elected?

A delegate from one of the small states, William Samuel Johnson of Connecticut, launched a heated debate with this observation: "A state exists as a political society, and it exists as a district of individual citizens. The aristocratic and other interests and the interests of the states must be armed with some power of self-defense. In one branch of the general government the people ought to be represented; in the other, the states."

Madison, Hamilton, and others argued, however, that the people should be represented in both branches, or houses.

When this single issue threatened to disrupt the proceedings, Madison sprang to his feet and cried out that "equal voice" in government by "unequal portions of the people is confessedly unjust," and would destroy the constitution "which we wish to last forever."

"A total separation of the states from each other, or partial confederacies, would alike be truly deplorable," Madison pleaded. "And those who may be accessory to either can never be forgiven by their country, nor by themselves."

Hamilton joined the fray. The Convention, he said, had reached the "critical moment" for forming a strong government. "It is a miracle that we are now here, exercising free deliberation," he said. "It would be madness to trust to future miracles. We must therefore improve the opportunity, and render the present system as perfect as possible."

Suddenly, by a vote of six to four, with one state divided, the method of election to the first branch was decided: Members of the first branch were to be elected by the people in proportion to the population of each state.

It was a decision that would never again be challenged.

Having lost their first battle for equal representation in the proposed government, the small states were determined to win the second.

Oliver Ellsworth of Connecticut moved that election of individuals to the second branch, or Senate, should be by the elected representatives of the states and not directly by the people. He hoped, he said, that the vote on the first branch would lead to "a grand compromise with regard to the second."

Then he warned: "On this middle ground, and on no other, can a compromise take place. If the great states refuse this plan, we shall be forever separated."

Since it was clear that Ellsworth spoke for all the small states, James Wilson of Pennsylvania promptly spoke up for the large states: "If the minority will have their own will and separate the union," Wilson said, "let it be done. I cannot consent that one-fourth shall control the power of three-fourths."

Ellsworth responded, "If the larger states seek security, they have it fully in the first branch. But are the lesser states equally secure? No. We are razing the foundation of the building when we need only repair the roof."

The diminutive Madison then said, "If there was real danger to the smaller states, I would give them defensive weapons. But there is none."

He then made this startling statement: "The real danger to our general government is that the northern and southern interests of the continent are opposed to each other, not from their difference of size, but from climate, and principally from the effects of their having or not having slaves."

The debate over representation in the Senate went on and on. Neither side, it appeared, was willing to give in.

Outside, it was muggy and very hot. Inside, with the windows tightly closed to maintain secrecy, the heat became almost unbearable. As the sweating delegates continued to argue, tempers flared. Nevertheless, Washington held the delegates to their task.

On June 28, just when it looked as if the Convention would collapse in failure, feeble

Benjamin Franklin made an unusual and sobering motion.

Addressing Washington, he said, "The small progress we have made after four or five weeks is, methinks, a melancholy proof of the imperfection of human understanding. We indeed seem to feel our own want of political wisdom, since we have been running about in search of it.

"In this situation, groping as it were in the dark to find political truth, how has it happened, sir, that we have not hitherto once thought of humbly applying to the Father of lights to illuminate our understanding?

"I have lived, sir, a long time, and the longer I live, the more convincing proofs I see of this truth, that God governs the affairs of men. And if a sparrow cannot fall to the ground without his notice, is it probable that an empire can rise without his aid?"

He then suggested that each session be opened with a prayer. Although the delegates believed in prayer, the motion failed. There was no money to pay a chaplain.

On several occasions, the disagreement over representation in the Senate again threatened to scuttle the Convention.

Toward the end of June, Oliver Ellsworth said bluntly that if the small states were not given equal voice in the Senate "we will be separated."

Madison and Wilson insisted, however, that such a decision would be "unjust." After several more hours of debate, Wilson reconsidered enough to suggest election of one member to the Senate for every 100,000 inhabitants, but not less than one member for the smaller states. Since the small states were so thinly populated, all knew this would still give the larger states a greater voice in the so-called second chamber.

"I make this proposal, not because I belong to a large state, but in order to pull down a rotten house and lay the foundation for a new building," Wilson said.

But the small states still balked. Franklin then added this philosophical note: "When a broad table is to be made and the edges of the planks do not fit, the artist takes a little from both, and makes a good joint. In like manner here, both sides must part with some of their demands in order that they may join in some accommodating proposition."

When neither side would yield, hefty Gunning Bedford of Delaware leveled a new blast at the large states, saying, "They insist they will never hurt or injure the lesser states. I do not, gentlemen, trust you!

"Where is your plighted faith?" he roared on. "Will you crush the smaller states? If the small states [join together], the fault will be yours and all the nations of the earth will justify us.

"We have been told with a dictatorial air that this is the last moment for a fair trial in favor of good government. It will be the last indeed, if the propositions reported from the committee go forth to the people!"

And then Bedford made the most ominous statement of all. "If the large states dissolve the confederation, the small ones will find some foreign ally of more honor and good faith who will take them by the hand."

A "foreign ally?" The delegates on both sides of the argument were shocked.

On July 2, the disgruntled delegates put the issue of equal representation in the so-called second branch to yet another vote. The result? The delegates of five states voted "aye" to the proposal made earlier by Oliver Ellsworth of Connecticut. Delegates to five others voted "no" while delegates representing one state—Georgia—were split. The convention was hopelessly deadlocked.

Now, Hugh Williamson of North Carolina told the Convention, "If we do not concede on both sides, our business must soon be at an end."

Washington, too, was distressed. "To please all is impossible, and to attempt it would be vain," he said.

He was relieved when South Carolina's Charles Pinckney rose in his seat and made this motion: "I propose that we appoint a grand committee of one member from each state to develop a sensible compromise."

Washington quickly called for a vote. "All in favor?"

"Aye!" came the unanimous response.

After the committee members were selected, Washington's gavel came down; the Convention was adjourned for July 4th, the nation's eleventh birthday.

For days, Washington's routine had been pretty much the same.

He rose early, breakfasted with the Morrises, then walked alone the one block to the State House, always arriving in time to get the proceedings underway at 10 o'clock. Adjournment was usually at 3 P.M. He then joined his friends in the taverns or in their private homes for dinner. On these occasions, the talk inevitably turned to developments in the State House. Always, Washington held to the same view: He wanted a strong central government put in place by the general public—rich or poor—and responsible to that public.

Occasionally, on a Sunday, Washington would ride out into the country. On the 4th of July, however, he went to church and later joined in the celebration of the signing of the Declaration of Independence.

When he returned to the chair in the State House a day later, the "grand committee" seemed to have found a solution to the impasse between the large and small states when it announced agreement on the following points:

• In the first chamber, the House of Representatives, each state would have one member for every forty-thousand in population, counting all the free inhabitants and three-fifths of the slaves. (The three-fifths formula was bitterly debated between those who would count all the slaves and those who refused to count any of them. Obviously the compromise gave the sparsely-settled southern states a greater voice in the House.)

• If a state had fewer than forty-thousand in population, it could seat one member in the first chamber. General Charles Cotesworth Pinckney of South Carolina, Charles Pinckney's older cousin, had reminded the delegates that the inhabitants of his state were "so sparse that four or five thousand men cannot be brought together to vote."

• The first chamber would have the authority to levy taxes, appropriate money, and fix the salaries of all members.

• Without being specific, the committee agreed that each state was to have an "equal vote" in the second branch.

The compromise was not totally accepted. James Wilson insisted that the committee had "exceeded its powers."

Alluding to the three-fifths formula applied to slaves and the "equal vote" in the Senate, Gouverneur Morris complained that "state attachments and state importance have been the bane of the country."

Morris, a fleshy man of thirty-five who banged awkwardly about on an exposed wooden left leg, was both brilliant and articulate in his speech.

"We cannot annihilate the serpents, but we may perhaps take out their teeth," he growled. "If persuasion does not unite the small states with the others, the sword will. The strongest party will make the weaker traitors and hang them. The larger states are the most powerful; they must decide."

White-haired George Mason of Virginia pleaded for "accommodation."

"It cannot be more inconvenient to any gentleman to remain absent from his private affairs than it is for me," Mason said. "But I will bury my bones in this city rather than expose my country to the consequences of a dissolution of the convention without anything being done!"

Another committee tried to find a solution to the many objections that were raised. And another. And another.

Washington became thoroughly disgusted. "Affairs are in a worse train than ever," he wrote to Alexander Hamilton, who had returned to New York briefly. "You can find but little ground on which the hope of a good establishment can be formed. I almost despair of seeing a favorable issue to the proceedings of our Convention, and do therefore repent having had any agency in this business."

Washington was justified in being discouraged. New Hampshire's full slate of two delegates had not arrived, Rhode Island still refused to participate, and two of New York's three delegates—Robert Yates and John Lansing Jr.—had gone home, convinced that the proposed Constitution was "destructive to the political happiness of the citizens of the United States." Their departure left only Alexander Hamilton to represent New York, a voice without a vote.

Suddenly, however, the tide turned. On July 16, when several delegates from the large states were absent, the small states managed to outvote their adversaries: The number of senators from each state was now set at two, and each senator was to have one vote.

Over the next week, there was rapid progress on a score of items. Agreement was reached on the judiciary, the admission of new states, and a tentative plan to elect the executive.

By July 26, twenty-three resolutions were in the hands of a five-man "committee on detail" that included Nathaniel Gorham, Oliver Ellsworth, James Wilson, Edmund Randolph, and John Rutledge. The five were given this charge: In ten days, organize the resolutions and put the first draft of the United States Constitution on paper!

Washington welcomed the ten-day interlude. On the 30th of July, he and Gouverneur Morris rode out to Valley Forge in Morris's phaeton, with his saddle horse towed behind.

Their destination was Mrs. Jane Moore's property, which lay along Trout Creek (now known as Valley Creek). After visiting Mrs. Moore, they set out for the pretty, winding stream for some leisurely fishing.

Even though the brown trout were plentiful and biting, Washington soon lost interest.

"I'm going to look around," he told Morris as he mounted one of the horses.

"Don't get lost," Morris joked.

Washington laughed and rode off.

The beauty of Valley Forge surprised him. The woods on the hilltops were all leafed out and the fields were under cultivation or covered with wildflowers and tall, green grasses.

He had been to the area only once; when he camped there with his troops during the winter of 1777–78. During most of that time the trees were bare, the ground was covered with snow, and it was bitterly cold.

In minutes, Washington was flooded with memories, for there in front of him, decaying and covered with weeds, were scores of the little huts his men had built to protect themselves from the frigid, snowy weather. And down in the valley, he could still see the little stone house he had used for headquarters. No one, it seemed, lived there now.

Nearby was the deserted bake house, which had often been used for meetings. Riding closer, he noticed that the front door was open and hanging askew and that a fallen tree had penetrated the roof.

At Christmas that awful winter, 11,000 starving men were encamped in Valley Forge, with only 8,000 fit for duty, and they only barely.

Two days before Christmas, Washington's Order of the Day had read, "Our want of provisions increases and disaffection is beyond belief. Since July we have had no assistance from the Quartermaster General.

"Few men have more than one shirt, many only the fragments of one, and some not at all."

In pleading to Congress and the states for help, one of Washington's letters began, "Without arrogance or the smallest deviation from the truth it may be said that no history now extant can furnish an instance of an army's suffering such uncommon hardships as ours have done. To see men without clothes to cover their nakedness, without blankets to lie on, without shoes, by which their marches may be traced by the blood of their feet."

The ride about Valley Forge reminded him that during February, the worst month, Martha, for the second time, had made the dangerous journey from Virginia to join him in the place he had chosen for winter quarters.

Then, too, that was the winter he discovered that two of his generals and others were plotting to unseat him. It was also the time a host of foreign officers had joined the American cause, notably drillmaster Baron von Steuben and later the young Marquis de Lafayette.

He rode over the old parade ground, where the great celebration was held in May 1778 when it was announced that France had become America's ally.

Nearby, he discovered a farmer working in a field of buckwheat. He asked the farmer how he raised and used this crop.

After tea at Mrs. Moore's, he returned to Philadelphia and noted in his diary that the Pennsylvania farmers used buckwheat as feed for cattle. It could also "lay fat on hogs" and when mixed with Irish potatoes was "very good for colts that are weaning."

Mount Vernon, as always, was very much on his mind.

Slavery: Like a time bomb, this inflammatory topic ticked away in the State House all through that hot and muggy summer of 1787. And for good reason. Seventy-four years before the Civil War, with some four million blacks in bondage (mostly in the South), slavery was already a divisive issue in America. There were abolition societies all over the North. Benjamin Franklin was president of one; Alexander Hamilton and John Jay were officers in another.

Scores of newspapers and virtually all churches were opposed to slavery. The Presbyterian synod, meeting in Philadelphia at the same time as the Convention, passed a resolution "to procure eventually the final abolition of slavery in America."

There were prominent southerners, too, who wished to bring an end to slavery. Among them were Washington, Richard Henry Lee, James Madison, Thomas Jefferson, and George Mason, all from Virginia, and all of whom owned slaves they had inherited.

Three elements of the slave issue were hotly debated off and on throughout the Convention:

• Should slaves be counted for purposes of representation in the House of Representatives?

• Should the proposed government of the United States continue to allow the importation of slaves from Africa?

• Should slave owners be allowed to pursue runaway slaves across the boundaries of free states and recapture them?

In August, the ticking bomb exploded.

"Upon what principle is it that the slaves shall be computed in the representation [to the House of Representatives]?" Gouverneur Morris cried, stamping his peg leg on the floor for emphasis. "Are they men? Then make them citizens and let them vote! The admission of slaves into the representation comes to this: that the inhabitant of Georgia and South Carolina who goes to the Coast of Africa, and in defiance of the most sacred laws of humanity, tears away his fellow creatures from their dearest connections and damns them to the most cruel bondages, shall have more votes in a government instituted for the protection of mankind than the citizen of Pennsylvania or New Jersey who views with a laudable horror so nefarious a practice."

Luther Martin of Maryland moved that the slave trade should be prohibited or subject to import taxes. "As five slaves are to be counted as three free men in the apportionment of representatives [to the first branch], such a clause weakens one part of the union which other parts are bound to protect," Martin pointed out. "It is also inconsistent with the principles of the Revolution and is dishonorable to the American character."

John Rutledge of South Carolina was quick to answer. "Religion and humanity have nothing to do with this question," he said. "Interest alone is the governing principle with nations. The true question at present is whether the southern states shall or shall not be parties to the Union."

Oliver Ellsworth of Connecticut, who had always favored states' rights, did so again. "Let every state import what it pleases," he said. "The morality or wisdom of slavery are considerations belonging to the states themselves."

Roger Sherman, also of Connecticut, said he was opposed to the slave trade, but "as the states are now possessed of the right to import slaves, and as it is expedient to have as few objections as possible to the proposed scheme of government, I think it best to leave the matter as we find it."

Charles Pinckney of South Carolina, the youngest delegate at twenty-nine, bluntly warned the delegates against tampering with the slave trade. "South Carolina can never receive the plan if it prohibits the slave trade," he said ominously. "In every proposed extension of the powers of Congress, that state has expressly and watchfully excepted that of meddling with the importation of negroes. If the states are all left at liberty on this subject, South Carolina may, perhaps, by degrees do of herself what is wished, as Virginia and Maryland have already done." (That is, quit the slave trade.)

Now the delegates heard from one of the most vocal opponents of slavery, George Mason of Virginia. "This infernal traffic [in slaves] originated in the avarice of British merchants," he raged. "The present question concerns not the importing states alone, but the whole Union! The western people are already calling out for slaves for their new lands, and will fill that country with slaves if they can be got through South Carolina and Georgia.

"I hold it essential in every point of view that the general government should have the power to prevent the increase of slavery."

John Dickinson of the small state of Delaware joined the debate with this statement: "On every principle of honor and safety it is inadmissible that the importation of slaves should be authorized to the states by the Constitution. The true question is whether the national happiness will be promoted or impeded by the importation; and this question ought to be left to the national government, not to the states particularly interested.

"I cannot believe," Dickinson concluded, "the southern states will refuse to join the new government on that account."

Dickinson's hopes were dashed when John Rutledge responded, "If the Convention thinks that North Carolina, South Carolina, and Georgia will ever agree to the plan, unless their right to import slaves be untouched, the expectation is in vain. The people of those states would never be such fools as to give up so important an interest."

Gouverneur Morris then calmed the Convention by making a motion to submit the slave-trade issue and other clauses pertaining to taxes on exports and imports and a commerce act to a committee for recommendations. "These things may form a bargain among the northern and southern states," he said placatingly. Morris's message was clear: To save the Union, compromise!

Despite protests from Sherman and Ellsworth, the Morris motion carried seven to three. Temporarily, at least, the crisis was averted.

There were eleven members on the new compromise committee. On August 25th, they had, as Gouverneur Morris hoped, struck a bargain.

Favored by the North were these principal agreements:

• Congress could pass any navigation or commerce law by a simple majority.

• No slaves could be imported after the year 1800.

• There would be an import tax on slaves, but it would be no higher than ten dollars a head.

These were favored by the South:

• For purposes of state representation and taxes, a ratio of five slaves to three free white inhabitants would be counted.

• Exports could not be taxed.

When the compromise was presented, Charles Pinckney moved that the cutoff date for the importation of slaves be extended to

1808. Since New England shipowners profited from transporting slaves, he was quickly seconded by Nathaniel Gorham of Massachusetts. The motion carried without dissent.

As the discussion went on, Pierce Butler of South Carolina suddenly rose and made this motion:

"If any person bound to service or labor in any of the United States shall escape into another state he or she shall be delivered up to the person justly claiming their service or labor."

Although the word "slave" was not mentioned, the clause meant that slave owners could cross into a free state, claim runaways, and have them "delivered up," presumably by local authorities. This clause also carried without dissent.

With slavery prohibited in the northern states and an end being brought to the importation of slaves in twenty years, many delegates were convinced that slavery would die out.

As Oliver Ellsworth put it, "Slavery in time will not be a speck in our country." Tragically, history would prove Ellsworth and others wrong.

The weary delegates decided to put the changes made by the committee of eleven to a formal vote.

Washington now had the arduous and tedious task of presiding over floor debates and ruling on such things as:

• The admission of foreign-born citizens to the legislature

• The origin of bills to appropriate money

• The handling of state debts

• National defense

• Treaties with other nations

• Creation of the judiciary

• The size of the army and the establishment of a navy

• The definition of treason

• The status of state militias

• How the new Constitution, when completed, was to be ratified by the states

• The seat of the new government (It was agreed that the "federal district" would not exceed "ten miles square," but its location was left to the legislature.)

• When and how often Congress should meet

• Who should preside over the Senate

Day after day, these and many other matters were discussed, voted on, rejected, or deferred as the delegates went over the proposed Constitution line by line.

Anxious to reach the end, Washington extended the hour of adjournment to 4 o'clock each day and added Saturdays to the schedule.

With this heavy workload, Washington declined almost all social invitations and spent every evening at the Morris house, entering quietly and going immediately to his rooms. During the evenings he studied the proposals and, occasionally, wrote letters to Martha, his farm manager, and his friends.

Significantly, a letter to Lafayette revealed his state of mind when he wrote, "There are seeds of discontent in every part of the Union, ready to produce other disorders if the wisdom of the present convention should not be able to devise, and the good sense of the people be found ready to adopt, a more vigorous and energetic government."

America, he felt, was still in danger.

By September, the Convention appeared to be in agreement on all articles of the Constitution except for one: the executive.

Who should select the head of the executive branch? The people? The state legislatures? Electors? One or both branches of the national legislature?

Should there be one, two, or three members of the executive branch? Was there to be a limit to age? Length of term? Who was eligible? How much power should it have in times of war and peace?

This issue, which had first surfaced in July, sparked just as many opinions as there were delegates.

When it was proposed that the election of the executive be made by the "national legislature" (Congress), Gouverneur Morris wanted nothing to do with it. He exploded, "An election by the national legislature will be the work of intrigue, of cabal, of corruption, and of faction."

And when it was moved that the election of the executive should be made by the people, George Mason said, "To refer the choice of a proper character for a chief magistrate to the people would be as unnatural as to refer a trial of colors to a blind man!"

While in committee of the whole, the delegates finally voted that a national executive should be a single individual chosen from the national legislature for a period of seven years and ineligible for a second term.

Washington, Gouverneur Morris, Madison, Wilson, and Gerry were opposed. Morris spoke for this group when he said, "Of all the possible modes of appointing the executive, an election by the people is the best; an election by the legislature is the worst. I prefer a short period with reeligibility but a different mode of election."

On September 3, debate on the executive was resumed. This time, it took only four days to reach agreement. The executive, it was decided, would be put in office by electors from each state; the term of office was set at four years, and reelection was possible for an unlimited number of terms.

The draft Constitution with all its revisions now went to a committee to "revise the style of and arrange the articles agreed to by the House."

On September 12, the committee submitted a Constitution with the following new titles and terms:

• The "first branch" of the legislature was designated as the House of Representatives.

• The "second branch" was to be called the Senate.

• The "court of last resort" was designated as the Supreme Court of the United States.

• The chief executive would be known as President of the United States of America.

When Washington recognized Edmund Randolph on the morning of Saturday, September 15, he assumed Randolph was about to make a motion to close the Convention. He was wrong.

Holding aloft a sheaf of papers, Randolph said, "The states should have the right to amend the Constitution in its present form. These amendments, together with the Constitution, should be submitted to another general Convention for a final decision. If not, I cannot sign the Constitution."

The stunned delegates, worn out by four months of tedious and often contentious debate, roared a protest. After Washington restored order, George Mason was recognized. Many thought he would censure Randolph. They, too, were wrong.

"I second the motion," Mason said grimly.

"This government, as established by the Constitution, will surely end either in a monarchy or a tyrannical aristocracy," he added. "This Constitution has been formed without the knowledge or idea of the people. A second Convention will know more of the sense of the people. It is improper to say to the people, take this or nothing.

"As it now stands, I can neither give it my support in Virginia nor sign it here. With the expedient of another Convention, I could sign."

Elbridge Gerry joined in, saying he still had eleven objections to the Constitution. After ticking them off, he said, "All of these I could get over if there were a second general Convention."

If the delegates refused to authorize a second convention, Gerry said, he, too, would not sign the Constitution.

Washington, determined to bring the Convention to a close, kept the delegates in the hall for seven hours without food or drink as the debate continued.

Late in the day, Charles Pinckney seemed to sum up the attitude of most when he said that he objected to some sections in the Constitution, "But, apprehending the danger of a general convulsion and an ultimate decision by the sword, I shall give it my support!"

Soon thereafter, Washington addressed the house. "On the proposition for another Convention, how do you say?" he asked.

On the roll call of the states, a majority boomed a unanimous "No!"

He then asked whether the delegates favored the Constitution in its present form.

The majority answered with a ringing "Aye!"

Only thirty-nine of the original fifty-five delegates were present for the final day of the Convention. And that morning, Benjamin Franklin asked James Wilson to read a speech Franklin had written for the occasion.

"Mr. President," Wilson read, "I confess that there are several parts of this Constitution which I do not at present approve. But I am not sure I shall never approve them. For having lived long, I have experienced many instances of being obliged by better information or fuller consideration, to change opinions even on important subjects, which I once thought right, but found to be otherwise. The older I grow, the more apt I am to doubt my own judgement, and to pay more respect to the judgement of others."

Most men, Franklin had written, think "themselves in possession of all truth."

That reminded him of "a certain French lady" who said during an argument with her sister, "I don't know how it happens, sister, but I meet with nobody but myself, that's always in the right."

Franklin said in his speech that he was "astonished" to find the Constitution so near to perfection.

"And I think it will astonish our enemies," he added, "who are waiting with confidence to hear that our councils are confounded and that our states are on the point of separation, only to meet hereafter for the purpose of cutting one another's throats."

Franklin approved of the Constitution because "I expect no better and because I am not sure that it is not the best."

"The opinions I have had of its errors," he went on, "I sacrifice to the public good. I have never whispered a syllable of them abroad. Within these walls they were born, and here they shall die."

In conclusion, Franklin said he hoped the delegates would "act heartily and unanimously in recommending the Constitution" and not "air their objections" to it publicly.

Later, he suggested this final compromise be added to the Constitution after Article VII:

"Done in Convention by the Unanimous Consent of the States present the Seventeenth Day of September in the Year of Our Lord one thousand seven hundred and eighty seven and of the Independence of the United States of America the twelfth . . ."

The wording, "by unanimous consent of the states . . . ," cleverly hid the discouraging fact that Randolph, Mason, and Gerry still refused to sign the Constitution.

Lining up behind Washington, in geographical order starting with New Hampshire, the thirty-eight others officially representing twelve of the thirteen states put their signatures beneath the text of the unprecedented document. Among them was Alexander Hamilton, the lone delegate from New York, who signed as an individual.

That night, Washington wrote in his diary: "The business being closed, the members ad-

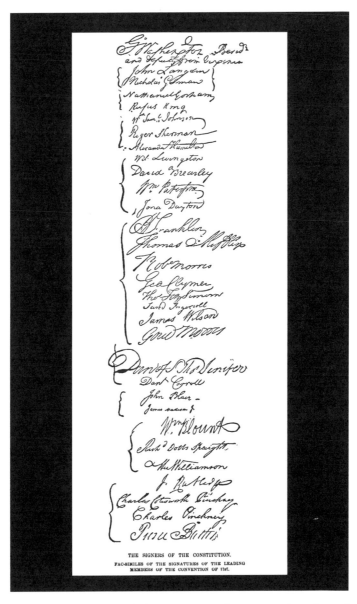

THE SIGNERS OF THE CONSTITUTION.

FAC-SIMILES OF THE SIGNATURES OF THE LEADING
MEMBERS OF THE CONVENTION OF 1787.

Although three delegates to the Constitutional Convention refused to sign the finished document, enough did to make it official.

journed to City Tavern, dined together, and took a cordial leave of each other; after which I returned to my lodgings to meditate on the momentous work which had been executed."

To become the law of the land the Constitution now had to be accepted by Congress, then sent on to be ratified by any nine States, which would make the two-thirds majority required by the Convention.

Only then could any meaning be given to these words: "We the People of the United States, in Order to form a more perfect Union, to establish Justice, insure domestic Tranquility, provide for the common defence, promote the general Welfare, and secure the Blessings of Liberty to ourselves and our Posterity, do ordain and establish this Constitution for the United States of America."

And only then could "the people" of the United States put a new government in place by electing their representatives, including their first president.

Book Two

While Benjamin Franklin was waiting in line to sign the Constitution on September 17, 1787, he pointed at the sturdy, high-backed chair George Washington had occupied throughout the proceedings; a chair that had a bright gold sun painted on its back.

"I have often in the course of the session, and the vicissitudes of my hopes and fears, looked at that behind the president without knowing whether that sun was rising or setting," he said with tears in his eyes. "But now I have the happiness to know it is a rising sun."

A few days later, the *Pennsylvania Packet* said, "In 1775 we beheld Washington at the head of the armies of America, arresting the progress of British tyranny. In 1787, we behold him at the head of a chosen band of patriots and heroes, arresting the progress of American anarchy, and taking the lead in laying a deep foundation for preserving that liberty by a good government, which he acquired for his country by his sword." Not everyone agreed with the lofty sentiments of Franklin and the *Packet,* however.

When the Constitution arrived at Congress in New York, an explanatory letter, signed by Washington was attached. It read:

"We kept steadily in view the consolidation of our union, in which is involved our prosperity, felicity, safety, perhaps our national existence. And thus this Constitution which we now present is the result of that mutual deference and concession which the peculiarity of our political situation rendered indispensable."

When distributed, the Constitution was promptly attacked by Richard Henry Lee of Virginia and the delegates representing New York.

The fifty-five-year-old Lee was a powerful political figure. A signer of the Declaration of Independence, he was a close friend of John and Samuel Adams and Patrick Henry. Congress, Lee shouted, could not support a measure that would put itself out of existence.

"And where," he went on while holding the Constitution above his head, "is the contract between the nation and the government? The Constitution makes mention only of those who govern, and nowhere speaks of the right of the governed."

Lee said he wanted to "qualify the immense power of the government" by including a "bill of rights," which was always seen as preserving the safety of a "free people" and was included in the constitutions of eight states.

The bill of rights would include mandates for:

- Rights of conscience
- Freedom of the press
- Trial by jury
- Prohibition of standing armies
- Freedom of elections
- Independent judges
- Security against excessive bails, fines, or punishments
- Security against unreasonable searches, and seizure of private property or papers
- The right of petition

Lee also called for immediate amendments to the Constitution that would, among other things, eliminate the vice presidency and increase representation.

Later, Lee, who believed that the Articles of Confederation provided for all the government the nation needed, offered a resolution that denied the Confederated Congress the power to approve the Constitution and to send it to the states for ratification. It was defeated twelve to one.

Congress then called on the states to hold ratification conventions as quickly as possible. Nevertheless, Lee's opening salvo in Congress signaled trouble ahead.

Without waiting to hear from Congress, Benjamin Franklin and his seven fellow delegates presented the Constitution to the Pennsylvania legislature on September 18, the day after it was signed. They hoped Pennsylvania would be the first state to ratify.

"We believe," the aged and ill Franklin said in a quavering voice, "this Constitution will produce happy effects for the Commonwealth of Pennsylvania as well as to every other state."

Thomas Mifflin, a Convention delegate, then read the Constitution aloud. As he did so, there were murmurs of disapproval. The new U.S. Constitution, the legislators realized, was markedly different from the Pennsylvania Constitution, of which many of them were quite proud.

After a ten-day delay, an impatient George Clymer, another Convention delegate, moved for the organization of a ratification convention.

The aging Benjamin Franklin knew that the Constitution was not perfect, but he believed it was the best that could be achieved.

"What's the hurry?" a belligerent member from a western county asked. "Not one in twenty outside Philadelphia knows anything about this Constitution. And what about Congress up there in New York? What do they say?"

Someone else suggested that since an election was to be held in November it might be wise to wait until the new assembly was seated.

After more argument, Robert Whitehill of Carlisle rose and said, "I move we postpone the question until four o'clock to afford those of us from the western counties time for reflection." The motion was seconded and approved.

At four o'clock, however, nineteen members were absent. The assembly was without a quorum.

"Go and find them," the sergeant-at-arms was told. Returning, he said, "They're locked in their lodgings at Mr. Boyd's on Sixth Street and refuse to come."

Philadelphia was a city of mostly artisans and mechanics. These workers favored the new Constitution because they realized it would help foreign trade and with it, their livelihood. When they heard ratification might fail in Pennsylvania, many were outraged and, meeting at Boyd's, had decided to take matters into their own hands.

The next morning, a mob broke into Boyd's rooming house, collared two of the assemblymen, carted them to the State House a short distance away and forced them into their seats.

"We now have a quorum!" a member of the mob shouted gleefully.

Just then, William Bingham, a delegate to Congress, arrived from New York and rushed up the aisle to the center of the room.

"I have here in my hand," he shouted above the noise of the delegates, "a copy of a resolution unanimously approved by Congress. It recommends that each state hold a convention as soon as possible to consider the Constitution as submitted!"

On a vote of forty-five to two, a ratification convention was scheduled to be held in Philadelphia on November 21st.

On returning to Mount Vernon, Washington sent copies of the Constitution to three former governors of Virginia: Patrick Henry, Benjamin Harrison, and Thomas Nelson. To each, he included a letter with identical wording that said in part:

"I wish the Constitution which is offered had been made more perfect, but I sincerely believe it is the best that could be obtained at this time; and, as a constitutional door is opened for amendment hereafter, the adoption of it under the present circumstances of the Union is, in my opinion, desirable.

"From a variety of concurring accounts it appears to me that the political concerns of this country are, in a manner, suspended by a thread," he added.

In conclusion, he noted that if "nothing had been agreed on" by those who attended the Constitutional Convention "anarchy would have soon ensued, the seeds being richly sown in every soil."

Harrison and Henry were unimpressed. Both said they would not support the Constitution as presented.

That put six of Virginia's most powerful political leaders—Harrison, Henry, George Mason, Edmund Randolph, Richard Henry Lee, and Colonel William Grayson (a Virginia delegate to Congress and a Lee ally)—clearly in the same camp. And all were quite vocal in their opposition to the Constitution.

Lee, for example, objected to "the greatness of the powers given and the multitude of military men, aristocrats, and drones, whose noise, impudence, and zeal exceeded all belief!"

Colonel Grayson, for his part, said the Constitution was a "most ridiculous piece of business formed by jumbling a number of ideas together. The temper of America is changed beyond conception." Ratification of the Constitution now seemed unlikely in the state that gave it birth.

What then, Washington wondered, were the chances for approval in other states?

As the political process sparked by Congress moved slowly forward in each state, Washington stuck doggedly to the continuing task of supervising the care of his five farms, the ferry, the mill, the manor house, and the fishery.

"I have not been ten miles from home since my return from Philadelphia," he said repeatedly in the steady stream of correspondence he sent friends around the country. In these letters, however, Washington was clear about his views:

• The Constitution might have faults, but it was the best that could be achieved under the circumstances.

• Nothing could be gained by another Constitutional Convention.

• If the Constitution were to be rejected, the nation would drift into ruin.

• But, he asked, what were people thinking and saying?

- Would the states ratify?
- Would they first insist on amendments?
- How many states favored another Constitutional Convention?
- How many demanded that a Bill of Rights be added?
- Among the leaders, who favored the Constitution? Who was opposed?

From all quarters came the answers.

Henry Knox wrote from Massachusetts that the Constitution was "received with great joy by all the commercial part of the community."

A writer to the *Pennsylvania Herald* said that "the arguments are that if the plan is not a good one, it is impossible that either General Washington or Doctor Franklin would have recommended it."

Another writer asked, "Is it possible that the deliverer of our country would have recommended an unsafe form of government for that liberty, for which he had for eight long years contended?"

The *Connecticut Courant,* in a story from Philadelphia, said "the Federalists would be distinguished hereafter by the name of Washingtonians, and the Anti-Federalists by the name of Shayites," a reference to Daniel Shays.

There was, however, bitter opposition. In the *Philadelphia Gazeteer,* a writer who called himself "Centinel" said, "Citizens! You have the culiar felicity of living under the most perfect system of local government in the world. Suffer it not to be wrested from you."

Centinel, in another article, said the "wealthy and ambitious" were attempting to seize control of the country, adding, "They have lulled all distrust and jealousy of their new plan by gaining the concurrence of the two men in whom America has the highest confidence."

Obviously referring to George Washington and Benjamin Franklin, Centinel went on to say that "the goodness and zeal of one has been imposed on, in a subject of which he must be necessarily inexperienced."

The other individual, said Centinel, suffered from "the weakness and indecision attendant on old age."

While Centinel continued his attacks through 1787 and on into early 1788, Washington was pleased by a brilliant and long series of widely circulated essays supporting the Constitution signed "Publius" and later "The Federalist." Most were written by Alexander Hamilton and some by John Jay and James Madison.

In what may well have been the most eloquent and persuasive speech offered by the Federalists, as supporters of the Constitution came to be known, James Wilson rose from his seat in the Pennsylvania State House and said, "The United States exhibits to the world the first instance of a nation unattacked by external force, unconvulsed by domestic insurrections, assembling voluntarily, deliberating fully, and deciding calmly concerning that system of government under which they and their posterity shall live."

Wilson said that putting the Constitution together was a difficult task "without precedent or guide."

"The United States contain already thirteen governments mutually independent," he pointed out. "Their soil, climates, productions, dimensions, and numbers [of inhabitants] are different. In many instances a difference and even an opposition subsists among their interests, and is imagined to subsist in many more."

"Mutual concessions and sacrifices were indispensably necessary to the success of the great work," he added.

He said that since states and citizens were represented in the Constitution it offered a "kind of liberty" that was unknown anywhere in the world.

"I shall distinguish it by the appellation of 'federal liberty,'" he said.

After explaining how the Constitution worked, he added, "Oft have I marked with silent pleasure and admiration the force and prevalence through the United States of the principle that the supreme power resides in the people, and that they never part with it.

"There can be no disorder in the community but may here receive a radical cure. Error in the legislature may be corrected by the Constitution; error in the Constitution by the people. The streams of power run in different directions, but they originally flow from one abundant fountain. In this Constitution, all authority is derived from the people."

When Wilson finished, the Anti-Federalists complained that the Constitution did not include a Bill of Rights and insisted that amendments should be added before it was adopted.

The debate, closely followed by Washington, went on for five weeks. Then, like a bolt out of the blue, came this electrifying news: "The deputies of the people of Delaware state fully, freely, and entirely approved of, assented to, ratified, and confirmed the Federal Constitution."

On December 7, 1787, only hours after the Delaware vote, Pennsylvania became the second state to ratify the Constitution, doing so by a vote of forty-six to twenty-three.

Eleven days later, when James Wilson appeared at an outdoor rally in Carlisle in support of the Constitution, he was attacked by a mob and clubbed to the ground.

Some said Wilson would have been killed if a former Continental soldier had not thrown himself over Wilson's body and absorbed many of the blows.

Despite similar bitter opposition, the Constitution was approved in New Jersey on December 18, in Georgia on January 2, 1788, and in Connecticut on January 9.

Now, Washington and others focused attention on Massachusetts. James Madison, sitting with Congress in New York, wrote, "The decision of Massachusetts either way will involve the result in New York."

John Langdon of New Hampshire also reported that if Massachusetts were to ratify, both his state and Rhode Island were sure to follow.

"If Massachusetts refuses to ratify, the Constitution will fail," Washington wrote to a friend glumly.

Massachusetts, long steeped in the tradition of town meetings, sent 355 delegates to the State House in Boston for the ratification convention, only to find that the building was too small to hold them.

The meeting then moved to the Brattle Street church, where it remained for a month as all sides of the issue were thoroughly thrashed out.

The delegates included farmers, ministers, mechanics, wealthy merchants, judges, senators, lawyers, sheriffs, shipowners, and landowners. And among those from the west were twenty-nine men who had fought with Daniel Shays. While there was a wide range of opinion about the Constitution, most of it was negative.

William Widgery of Maine (Maine was then part of Massachusetts) was especially indignant about the proposal that Congress should have the power to "lay and collect taxes."

"Who, sir, is to pay the debts of the yeomanry and others?" he asked hotly. "All we hear is that the merchant and farmer will flourish, and that the mechanics and tradesmen are to make their fortunes directly, if the Constitution goes down. Sir, when oil will quench fire, I will believe all this, and not till then.

"Some gentlemen have given out that we are surrounded by enemies, that we owe debts, and that the nations will make war against us and take our shipping. Sir, I ask, is that a fact?"

Another delegate complained that there was no provision in the Constitution that "men of power should have any religion.

"A Papist or an infidel is as eligible as a Christian!" he snorted.

Samuel Nason, a storekeeper and saddler from Maine, railed against the provision for a standing army.

"Had I a voice like Jove," he said, "I would proclaim it throughout the world. And had I an arm like Jove I would hurl from the world those villains that would attempt to establish in our country a standing army!"

To all of the objections and questions, those who signed the Constitution—Fisher Ames, Nathaniel Gorham, Rufus King, and Caleb Strong—gave patient and considerate answers.

Occasionally, however, a delegate would respond to a complaint. When Amos Singletary, a farmer who had never gone to school, insisted that the "lawyers and men of learning, and moneymen" expected to get into Congress and "get all the power and all the money into their own hands," he was answered by another farmer named Jonathan Smith.

Smith, who came from the area where Shays's Rebellion had taken place, said he was a "plain man" who made his living "by the plow."

"I am not used to speak in public," he said, "but I beg your leave to say a few words to my brother plow joggers. I have lived in a part of the country where I have known the worth of good government by the want of it. There was a black cloud that rose in the east last winter, and spread over the west."

He said he was ready to "snatch at anything that looked like a government."

"Now, Mr. President, when I saw this Constitution, I found that it was a cure for these disorders. I got a copy of it, and read it over and over. I had been a member of the convention to form our own state constitution, and had learnt something of the checks and balances of power, and I found them all there. I did not go to any lawyer to ask his opinion. We have no lawyer in our town, and do well enough without. I formed my own opinion, and was pleased with this Constitution."

He said the lawyers and moneymen Singletary had complained of were all "embarked on the same cause as us. We must sink or swim together.

"Some gentlemen say, don't be in a hurry; take time to consider, and don't take a leap in the dark," he said in conclusion. "I say, take things in time; gather fruit when it is ripe.

"There is a time to sow and a time to reap; we sowed our seed when we sent men to the federal convention; now is the harvest, now is the time to reap the fruit of our labor. And if we don't do it now, I am afraid we never shall have another opportunity."

When there was another protest against imports and excises, Thomas Dawes of Boston, a shipowner, said, "For want of general laws of prohibition through the union, our coasting trade, our whole commerce, is going to ruin. A vessel from Halifax [Canada] with its fish and whalebone find as hearty a welcome at the southern ports as though built and navigated and freighted from Salem [Massachusetts].

"South of Delaware, three-fourths of the exports and three-fourths of the returns are made in British [ships]," he added. "Of timber, one-half of the value, or other products shipped for London from a southern state, three-tenths go to the British carrier. This money belongs to the New England states, because we can furnish the ships much better than the British."

Dawes pointed out that under the Articles of Confederation, Congress had neither the authority nor the power to help American mills and manufacturers.

"If we wish to encourage our own manufacturers, to preserve our own commerce, to raise the value of our own lands, we must give Congress the powers in question," he concluded.

When there was a protest to the compromise over slavery, Dawes answered, "Congress in the year 1808 may wholly prohibit the importation of slaves, leaving every particular state in the meantime to its own option totally to prohibit their introduction into its own territories. Slavery could not be abolished by an act of Congress in a moment; but it has received a mortal wound."

The arguments went on and on. Finally, with a push from John Hancock and Samuel Adams, the convention voted and issued this statement: "[We acknowledge] with grateful hearts the goodness of the Supreme Ruler of the Universe in affording the people of the United States . . . an opportunity, deliberately and peaceably, without fraud or surprise, of entering into an explicit and solemn compact with each other, by assenting to and ratifying a new Constitution."

The vote was 187 to 168. Massachusetts ratified the Constitution by a margin of only nineteen votes.

Although six states—Connecticut, Massachusetts, Pennsylvania, Georgia, Delaware, and New Jersey—had ratified, Washington was concerned about the growing strength of Anti-Federalists in New York, Virginia, Maryland, and South Carolina.

Just as he had as commander in chief during the Revolution, he studied carefully the daily reports that poured into his "headquarters" at Mount Vernon. What he saw was this:

• Maryland and South Carolina were on the brink of making a decision. He hoped for ratification in both states. If he was right, that would mean only one more state need ratify to make the nine necessary for adoption of the Constitution.

• Looking at the calendar where he had noted the dates of the upcoming conventions, it appeared the ninth state could be either New York, New Hampshire, or Virginia.

During January, February, and March bad weather kept Washington housebound most of the time. During this period, with the help of his friend and former army aide David Humphreys, who had come for a long visit, he wrote letter after letter to Federalists in every state. Always, his message was the same: To save America, the Constitution must be ratified.

To Washington's dismay, John Langdon wrote that New Hampshire had postponed a vote until June.

Fearing that Maryland might do the same, Washington hurriedly wrote to his old friend, Governor Thomas Johnson.

"An adjournment of your convention will be tantamount to the rejection of the constituents," Washington warned. "Great use is made of the postponement in New Hampshire. An event similar to this in Maryland would have the worst tendency imaginable; for indecision there would certainly have considerable influence upon South Carolina, the only other state to precede Virginia."

Shortly after the Maryland convention got underway on April 21, one delegate proposed a plan for a confederacy of the slave-holding states. The plan was totally ignored.

Despite fierce opposition from three fiery Anti-Feds, as they were now called, Maryland ratified sixty-three to eleven, a margin of almost six to one.

E lated by the Maryland vote, Washington wrote Lafayette:

"It is impracticable for any one who has not been on the spot to realize the change in men's minds, and the progress toward rectitude in thinking and acting.

"The plot thickens fast. A few short weeks will determine the political fate of America for this present generation, and probably produce no small influence on the happiness of society through a long succession of ages to come.

"Should everything proceed with harmony and consent according to our actual wishes and expectations, it will be so much beyond anything we had a right to imagine or expect eighteen months ago that it will, as visibly as any possible event in the course of human affairs, demonstrate the finger of Providence."

Washington knew, however, that the slavery issue might once again raise its head in South Carolina; and this time seriously threaten ratification.

"When this new Constitution shall be adopted, the sun of the southern states will set, never to rise again! What cause is there for jealousy of our importing Negroes? Why confine us to twenty years? Why limit us at all? This trade can be justified on the principles of religion and humanity. They do not like our slaves in the North because they have none themselves, and therefore, want to exclude us from this great advantage."

These were the words of Rawlins Lowndes as he attacked the federal Constitution at a session of the South Carolina legislature in mid-January 1788, long before a convention was scheduled to consider the proposed government.

Lowndes, a former governor, spoke after Charles Pinckney had spent several hours going over the Constitution.

"The slave trade is prohibited in every state but Georgia and the two Carolinas," one of the legislators protested as Lowndes paused in his emotional harangue.

Ignoring the comment, Lowndes said, "Without Negroes, this state would degenerate into one of the most contemptible in the Union. Negroes are our wealth, our only natural resource; yet our kind friends in the North are determined soon to tie up our hands and drain us of what we have."

Charles Cotesworth Pinckney stoutly defended the efforts of the four South Carolina delegates who had attended the Constitutional Convention.

"Your delegates had to contend with the religious and political prejudices of the eastern and middle states, and the interested and inconsistent opinion of Virginia," he said.

"It was alleged that slaves increase the weakness of any state which admits them; that an invading enemy could easily turn them against ourselves and the neighboring states; and that, as we are allowed a representation for them, our influences in government would be increased in proportion as we were less able to defend ourselves."

He said a committee had been appointed to break the deadlock over the slavery issue "and did so after a great deal of difficulty."

He then pointed to the advantages to the South, saying, "We have secured an unlimited importation of Negroes for twenty years. The general government can never emancipate them, for no such authority is granted and it is admitted on all hands that the general government has no powers but what are expressly granted by the Constitution.

"We have obtained a right to recover our slaves in whatever part of America they may take refuge, which is a right we had not before."

"In short, we have made the best terms in our power for the security of this species of property," he concluded.

Now, Lowndes complained that the eastern states would dominate the House of Representatives and divest the South "of any pretensions to the title of a republic."

Edward Rutledge answered, "The fears that the northern interests will prevail at all times are ill-founded. Several of the northern states are already full of people; the migrations to the South are immense; in a few years, we shall rise high in our representation while other states will keep their present position."

Pinckney, knowing this issue was of real concern to many, added his thoughts. "We are weak," he admitted. "By ourselves we cannot form a union strong enough for the purpose of effectually protecting each other. Without union with the other states, South Carolina must soon fall.

"Is there any one among us so naive as to suppose that this state could long maintain her independence if she stood alone, or was only connected with the southern states?"

It was best to form a close union with the stronger eastern states which, with their navy, would serve the South in both peace and war, he said.

There was no more talk of slaves and power. By a unanimous vote, a convention was scheduled for May 13. And ten days after it opened, South Carolina adopted the Constitution by a vote of 149 to 73, a margin of two to one.

Washington was in the library at Mount Vernon with David Humphreys when Tobias Lear rushed in waving a document that had just been delivered by an express rider from the south.

"Number eight!" he shouted.

"South Carolina," Washington breathed as he scanned the papers Lear handed him. "One more and it will be done."

Then, with a note of wonder in his voice, he added: "Eight states have ratified without a negative; three of them unanimously. Six to one in another. Three to one in another. Two to one

Tobias Lear was Washington's longtime secretary.

in two more. Together, there should be enough weight to stamp out any opposition."

On cooler reflection, Washington admitted that the "opposition" was still very much alive, especially in Virginia, next in line to consider the Constitution.

"If Virginia fails to ratify," Washington said, "New York will follow suit."

"So will Rhode Island," Humphreys said.

"And North Carolina," Lear added.

I̶n 1788, Virginia was the largest of the thirteen states. It had one-fifth of the total population of the Union in a vast domain that embraced West Virginia and the District of Kentucky, and extended westward to the Mississippi River.

It also boasted several of the leading statesmen of the period, including Richard Henry Lee, James Monroe, James Madison, George Mason, Edmund Randolph, Benjamin Harrison, and the brilliant orator Patrick Henry.

Two of the greats, however, were missing as Virginia's ratification convention got underway in Richmond on June 12: Thomas Jefferson was in Paris as ambassador to France; and George Washington waited at Mount Vernon to learn whether his dream of a national government would come true.

The fireworks started early when Patrick Henry disregarded a resolution made by George Mason that the 168 delegates should first read the Constitution through before starting debate.

"'We the people?'" the fifty-two-year-old Henry sarcastically cried out to the delight of the packed gallery as the first line was read. "Who authorizes gentlemen to speak the language of 'We, the people,' instead of 'We, the states?' The people gave the convention no power to use their name!"

For three weeks the debate raged, with Henry, at one point, holding the floor for seven hours.

"Whither is the spirit of America gone?" he called out, his blue eyes flashing, his elongated, thin body quivering with passion.

"Whither is the genius of America fled? We drew the spirit of liberty from our British ancestors. But now, sir, the American spirit, assisted by the ropes, and chains of consolidation, is about to convert this country into a powerful and mighty empire.

"There will be no checks, no real balances in this government. What can avail your specious, imaginary balances, your rope-dancing, chain-rattling, ridiculous ideal checks and contrivances?" Henry thundered.

George Mason who, along with Edmund Randolph and Elbridge Gerry, had refused to sign the Constitution, added his considerable weight to the arguments of the Anti-Feds. Mason insisted that the Constitution would give America a "national" government, one that would destroy the liberties of the people.

"The power of laying direct taxes changes the confederation," he said. "The general government being paramount and more powerful, the state governments must give way to it; and a general consolidated government is one of the worst curses that can befall a nation."

Edmund Pendleton disagreed. "There is no quarrel between government and liberty," he said. "The former is the shield and protector of the latter. The expression 'we the people' is a common one and with me, a favorite. Who but the people can delegate powers, or have a right to form a government?

"Common danger, union, and the spirit of America carried us through the war, and not the confederation of which the moment of peace showed the imbecility of it.

"Government to be effective, must have complete powers, a legislature, a judiciary, and executive. No gentlemen in this committee would agree to vest these three powers in one body. The proposed government is not a consolidated government. It is a government of laws and not of men."

Later, Henry brought up another point. "In the British government the sword and purse are not united in the same hands; in this system they are," he said. "Does not infinite security result from a separation?"

Madison quickly responded, his voice low as usual, but listened to with respect. "There never was, and there never will be, an efficient government in which both the sword and purse are not vested, though they may not be given to the same member of government. The sword is in the hands of the British king; the purse in the hands of parliament. It is so in America as far as an analogy can exist.

"There is more responsibility in the proposed government than in the English," he said. "Our representatives are chosen for two years, in England for seven. Any citizen may be elected here; in Great Britain no one without an estate of the annual value of six hundred pounds sterling can represent a county. If confidence be due to the government there, it is due tenfold here."

Day by day and point by point, the delegates argued the merits of the Constitution. On the eleventh and the seventeenth of June, Mason raised questions about the agreement reached on slavery.

"The augmentation of slaves weakens the states," he said. "Such a trade is diabolical in itself and disgraceful to mankind; yet by this Constitution it is continued for twenty years. Much as I value a union of all the states, I would not admit the southern states into the union unless they agree to its discontinuance."

Madison calmly replied that he, too, abhorred slavery. But, he explained, "The gentlemen of South Carolina and Georgia argued, 'by hindering us from importing this species of property the slaves of Virginia will rise in value, and we shall be obliged to go to your markets.' I need not expatiate on this subject; great as the evil is, a dismemberment of the union would be worse."

In explaining the compromise reached on the slavery issue, he noted that under the Articles of Confederation the slave traffic could go on forever. The Constitution, however, would "put an end to it after twenty years."

While Madison was the most persuasive of the Federalists, Edmund Randolph surprised the convention by suddenly joining their ranks. He had, he admitted, refused to sign the Constitution because he felt it should be amended prior to adoption. To postpone the convention for that purpose "at this late date would be impossible without inevitable ruin to the Union.

"The question now is between union and no union," Randolph said, "and I would sooner lop off my right arm than consent to a dissolution of the union." He would favor the Constitution if it would include "subsequent amendments" as had been urged by Massachusetts.

Late in the day on June 25th, the Convention considered this resolution: Should the Constitution be ratified, referring "subsequent" amendments to the first Congress under the Constitution?

"Yes!"

With that vote (and New Hampshire's earlier the same day) Washington got his wish: America had become a nation.

D espite ratification by ten states, Washington was full of concern. After all, it was possible that three states could be left out of the Union.

Of the three, New York was by far the most important. It had been the scene of many critical events of the war—the battles of Long Island, Kip's Bay, Fort Washington, Saratoga, White Plains, and Stony Point, not to mention the thwarted treachery of Benedict Arnold at West Point.

Despite its history, however, Washington feared that New York might become an independent state along with Rhode Island and North Carolina.

"Imagine what it would mean if New York, with its harbors, lakes, rivers, and large population were to become independent or fall into hostile hands," he told Humphreys as they discussed the ongoing battle in New York.

"Hamilton will come through for us," Humphreys soothed. "And when New York ratifies, the others will, too."

Humphreys was right. Hamilton, with extraordinary vigor and skill, fought off the Anti-Feds led by Governor George Clinton (who was also president of the New York convention) as they struggled to add amendments before the Constitution was adopted.

Clinton insisted that his followers were "friends to the rights of mankind," while his opponents were "advocates of despotism."

In one of his most telling speeches, Hamilton responded to fears that the federal government would swallow the rights of the states and the people they represented by saying: "The establishment of a republican government on a safe and solid basis is the wish of every honest man in the United States, and is the nearest and dearest to my own heart.

"This great purpose requires strength and stability in the organization of the government, and vigor in its operations," he added. "State governments must form a leading principle. They can never lose their powers till the whole people of America are robbed of their liberties."

On July 27, New York ratified. The vote was close: 30 to 27, a margin of only three. Within the next two years, North Carolina and Rhode Island joined the parade, encouraged to do so by the promise of amendments.

Moving deliberately, the Confederated Congress had already set in motion the steps that would lead to the formation of the new government, including these:

• New York was selected as the temporary seat of government.

• On the first Wednesday in January 1789, each state was to choose presidential electors.

• On the first Wednesday in February, the electors were to meet and cast their votes.

• On the first Wednesday in March, the government would be launched under the terms spelled out in the Constitution.

The first president of the United States was soon to be chosen by the people.

Without a doubt, George Washington's influence and ghostlike presence at each state convention was mainly responsible for adoption of the Constitution.

As James Monroe was to write to Thomas Jefferson after the Virginia conclave: "Be assured, General Washington's influence carried this government."

Now, it appeared that virtually everyone in America had only one man in mind for the presidency: George Washington.

The *Pennsylvania Packet,* one of the most important newspapers in the country, repeatedly identified Washington—and no one else—as the man who would be president. And when the nation celebrated the signing of the Declaration of Independence on July 4th, 1788, it was seen in many towns as a call to Washington to accept the presidency.

In Wilmington, Delaware, for example, celebrants raised their glasses to "Farmer Washington, may he be called from the plow to rule a great people."

In Frederick, Maryland, there was this toast: "May the savior of America gratify the ardent wishes of his countrymen by accepting that post which the voice of mankind has assigned him."

In York, Pennsylvania, local citizens sang a song that closed several stanzas with these words:

"Great Washington shall rule the land
While Franklin's counsel aids his hand."

During a parade in New York on July 23, a float carried a uniformed figure identified as the "illustrious Washington, may he be the first president of the United States."

This movement became stronger on the occasion of Washington's fifty-sixth birthday, on February 22, 1789, celebrated with enthusiasm in many communities throughout the thirteen states.

Washington, however, had never even hinted that he wanted to be president; much less that he would campaign for it. Publicly, he remained silent on the issue. When friends broached the subject directly, he dodged it.

In September 1788, Hamilton had voiced the opinion of many when he told Washington: "In a matter so essential to the well-being of society as the prosperity of a newly instituted government, a citizen of so much consequence as yourself to the success has no option but to lend his services if called for."

In his response, Washington said, "If I should receive the appointment and if I should be prevailed upon to accept it, the acceptance would be attended with more diffidence and reluctance than I ever experienced before in my life." He had no wish, he often declared, "beyond the humble and happy lot of living and dying a private citizen on my own farm."

The votes of the electors confirmed in February, however, that the wishes of his countrymen were otherwise.

One report came from Henry Knox: "It appears by the returns of elections hitherto observed, which is as far as Maryland southward, that your Excellency has every vote for President and Mr. John Adams twenty-eight for Vice President."

While Washington made no comment during the election, he thought it best to be prepared. On March 4, he borrowed six hundred pounds from a wealthy man in Alexandria at six percent interest. This, he thought, would allow him to pay his taxes (the sheriff had called on him three times) and cover his expenses of traveling to New York.

On March 7, Washington journeyed to Fredricksburg with Martha to see his mother, who was about eighty years old and dying of breast cancer.

Thus, when Secretary of Congress Charles Thomson entered the banquet hall at Mount Vernon on that fateful April day in 1789, Washington knew he must serve.

"I bade adieu to Mount Vernon, to private life, and to domestic felicity, and with a mind oppressed with more anxious and painful sensations than I have words to express, set out for New York."

This melancholy entry in Washington's diary was written on April 16, in Alexandria, the first stop on his long, northward journey.

Clearly, Washington had serious concerns about his mission. Just before he closed the diary, put out the candles, and went to bed, he wrote that he was going to New York "with the best disposition to render service to my coun-

The "dove of peace" has graced the roof of Mount Vernon since the time Washington left his beloved home to take office as president.

try in obedience to its call, but with less hope of answering its expectations."

The public, however, had no such misgivings. Never before, or since, has an American, in any walk of life or field of endeavor, been so universally applauded, cheered, encouraged, lionized, and loved.

When Washington's carriage, with the president-elect, Charles Thomson, and David

Humphreys aboard, rolled over roads muddy and rutted by spring rains to the outskirts of Alexandria, a paean began that would last for days.

A large mounted escort met Washington's carriage and led the way into the town. When it reached the city streets, a band and a troop of soldiers, many of them veterans from his Revolutionary War army, fell in behind.

A huge crowd gathered along the route, cheering wildly as Washington, waving from the carriage window, passed by.

That evening, a dinner was given in Washington's honor and after the now obligatory thirteen toasts were tossed off, Mayor Dennis Ramsay again raised his glass and said, "Farewell! Go and make a grateful people happy, a people who will be doubly grateful when they contemplate this recent sacrifice for their interest.

"To that Being, who maketh and unmaketh at His will, we commend you; and, after the accomplishment of the arduous business to which you are called, may He restore to us again the best of men and the most beloved fellow-citizen."

Washington, filled with emotion, made a brief response that ended with, "from an aching heart, I bid you all, my affectionate friends and kind neighbors, farewell!"

onscious that Congress was waiting and impatient to launch the new government, Washington hoped to make a swift journey by starting at sunrise every day. It was not to be.

As he was about to leave Alexandria, he received a letter from a former brigadier general of the First Maryland Infantry, Otho Williams.

"To avoid as much as possible every circumstance which might occasion delay or solicit too much of Your Excellency's attention, the gentlemen [greeting him] would move in files and on meeting you will open right and left," Williams said thoughtfully. "And if Your Excellency will please pass through, they will wheel into the rear and follow your suite to town. The gentlemen also propose to have the honor of conducting Your Excellency out of town."

The "town" Williams referred to was Baltimore. When Washington arrived on the afternoon of April 17, he was greeted by another parade, touched off with a barrage of artillery fire.

At a dinner that evening, Washington was given copies of an address that bore the signatures of several heroes who had fought under him during the war.

"We behold," the speaker said, "a new era springing out of our independence and a field displayed where your talents for governing will not be obscured by the splendor of the greatest military exploits. We behold, too, an extraordinary thing in the annals of mankind; a free and enlightened people, choosing by a free election, without one dissenting voice, the late commander in chief of their armies to watch over and guard their civil rights and privileges."

Determined to travel as fast as possible, Washington was on the road the next morning at 5:30. But even that hour wasn't too early for his admirers. He left Baltimore to the sound of cannon and was, as promised by General Williams, escorted out of town by a large contingent of horsemen.

The greeting in Wilmington, Delaware, two days later was a repeat of that in Baltimore.

At Chester, Pennsylvania, there was a change in the routine for the trip to Philadelphia. A group of army veterans brought a white, caparisoned saddle horse for Washington and two bays for Thomson and Humphreys.

"We want everyone to be able to see Your Excellency when you arrive in the town," the leader of the welcoming committee explained.

Washington obediently rode to the front and once again entered the city where he had experienced victory and defeat and where so much of America's destiny had been shaped.

As he did so, the crowds of greeters swelled rapidly on all sides. And it soon became evident that Philadelphia had gone to extraordinary lengths to welcome its hero.

The arches to the bridge at Gray's Ferry, for example, were bedecked with laurel, while the ferryboats anchored in the stream flew colorful flags and banners.

And mounted along the sides of the bridge were more banners, many denoting the states that had ratified the Constitution, others carrying phrases like "The New Era" and "Don't Tread on Me."

As Washington rode under the western arch of the bridge, one newspaper reported, a girl in a white dress "lowered on the hero's brow a wreath of laurel." The child was identified as fifteen-year-old Angelica Peale, daughter of Charles Willson Peale, an artist who had painted Washington's portrait many times.

By the time Washington rode into the city proper, some 20,000 people were on hand to greet him. And, as the *Federal Gazette* reported, "private citizens" invited the clergy "and all respectable strangers" to a dinner for Washington at City Tavern.

The *Gazette* also reported that Washington remained at the dinner "to the very end and captured every heart."

Before he left Philadelphia, Washington wrote John Langdon, president of the Senate, to inform him of his plans.

"Knowing how anxious both houses must be to proceed to business, I shall continue my journey with as much dispatch as possible."

Unfortunately for the congressmen waiting in New York, Washington's adoring public had other plans.

On Tuesday, April 21, the day of his departure, five different committees called on him to make complimentary speeches. All required responses. Even though Washington had asked that there be no parades, he was escorted out of Philadelphia and beyond by a troop of horsemen.

At Trenton, New Jersey, which brought back memories of his first victory over the British that bitter Christmas Day 1776, he received another extraordinary greeting.

The bridge over Assunpink Creek had been covered with greenery, and a sign on the southern end proclaimed, "The Defender of the Mothers will also Defend the Daughters."

As he crossed the bridge, scores of young girls and women, mostly dressed in white, carried baskets of flowers and scattered them in his path. As they did so, they chorused:

Welcome, mighty Chief! once more
  Welcome to this grateful shore!
  Now no mercenary foe,
  Aims again the fatal blow—
  Aims at the fatal blow.

Virgins fair, and Matrons grave,
  Those thy conquering arms did save,
  Build for the triumphant bowers
  Strew ye fair, his way with flowers—
  Strew your Hero's way with flowers.

In a voice choked with emotion, Washington thanked the girls and women "for the great honor you have done me."

But after more honors in Princeton and New Brunswick, the greatest display of adulation was yet to come.

After meeting a congressional committee at Elizabeth, New Jersey, Washington, with the whole town on his heels, proceeded to the waterfront, where he was obliged to review a large body of soldiers drawn up near the dock.

He then boarded a forty-seven-foot barge equipped with a sail and a gaily decorated awning. The crew consisted of a coxswain and twenty-six oarsmen, all dressed in white smocks and wearing black, fringed caps.

When the barge shoved off, Washington heard an artillery salute from behind. With the help of a brisk following wind, his little vessel quickly crossed the waters that led to New York harbor. As it did so, it appeared that everything that could float fell in behind, each vessel festooned with banners and flags.

Soon, Washington saw another barge almost identical to his own. As the barges drew closer, he spotted his old friend Henry Knox, now secretary of foreign affairs, John Jay, and other officials. All exchanged joyous waves and shouts of greeting.

Suddenly, a sloop under full sail swept close to the barge. Several of the occupants, to the tune of "God Save the King," sang a song of praise directed at Washington.

Now, directly ahead and close to the shore of Manhattan, a score of vessels could be seen drifting or riding at anchor, all with flags flying from every mast and halyard.

At the Battery, the landing site, an immense crowd of citizens, soldiers, and dignitaries eagerly awaited Washington's arrival. When his barge landed, thousands of voices screamed a welcome, church bells rang, ships' horns and whistles were blown, and there was a thirteen-gun salute.

After stepping ashore, Governor George Clinton and a large committee greeted Washington warmly. When the exchanges seemed completed, an army officer stepped forward, saluted smartly, and announced that he was in command of the guard assigned to protect Washington.

"I await your orders, sir," the officer said. When the officer spoke, the crowd quieted to listen to what Washington might say.

After a look at the faces around him, Washington told the officer, "As to the present arrangement, I shall proceed as directed, but after this is over, I hope you will give yourself no further trouble as the affection of my fellow citizens is all the guard I want." This remark, repeated to those unable to hear it, brought tears to many eyes and cheers from all.

Because the crowd was so dense, it took nearly an hour for Washington to move from the dock to his new home at Number 3 Cherry Street, only a short distance away.

In the hours and days that followed, Congress wrestled with the problem of how, when, and where to conduct America's first inauguration. As they did so, Washington was obliged to attend a seemingly endless series of celebrations, dinners, and speeches. Finally, Congress decided that the inauguration would be held on the afternoon of April 30 in Federal Hall.

There was, however, a snag. The Senate and the House of Representatives couldn't agree on Washington's title. The Senate favored "His Highness, the President of the United States of America, and Protector of their Liberties." The House wished to stick to the wording used in the Constitution: "President of the United States." The House won. It was time to proceed.

New York awakened to the boom! boom! of cannon fire that cool and cloudy morning of April 30, 1789. Thirteen evenly spaced shots in all made a fitting salute to what would be an auspicious day in American history. By nine o'clock, when church bells rang throughout the city to summon people to prayer, the skies had cleared, and bright sunshine warmed the air.

In his quarters on Cherry Street, Washington, with the help of Humphreys and Tobias Lear, prepared himself for the big day, all the while regretting that Martha had decided to stay home with her grandchildren.

He dressed in a plain, brown broadcloth suit that had been made in Hartford, Connecticut, and purchased for him by Henry Knox. And with the metal buttons, which bore the likeness of an eagle with its wings spread, proclaiming "liberty," the suit clearly said "Made in America."

Washington also wore white silk stockings and black shoes adorned with well-polished silver buckles. To complete this simple costume, he fastened a dress sword in a steel scabbard to his waist.

Shortly after noon, eight members of a joint committee of Congress arrived to escort him to Federal Hall, south of Wall Street. On entering the house on Cherry Street, the chairman, Senator Ralph Izard, said simply, "Congress is ready to receive you, Your Excellency."

During the short trip, Washington rode alone in a sumptuous carriage pulled by four handsome horses in gleaming harness. Lear and Humphreys followed close behind in Washington's carriage.

Well aware of what was taking place, hundreds of New Yorkers clogged the narrow streets, forcing the procession to move slowly and carefully.

The two houses of Congress were waiting for Washington in the Senate chamber, a handsome, newly decorated room that measured forty feet by thirty feet and featured a ceiling painted with the sun and stars.

As Washington walked from a door at the back of the room toward a platform and three chairs at the front, he found the Senators on his right and the members of the House on his left. All were standing and applauding politely.

John Adams, who had been elected vice president, greeted him at the platform along with Frederick Muhlenberg, the speaker of the House.

Following directions given earlier, Washington sat in the center chair. Muhlenberg then took the chair on his left, Adams the one on his right. Now, Congress, with much scuffling and scraping of feet, became seated.

After a long moment of silence, John Adams rose and said solemnly, "Sir, the Senate and the House of Representatives are ready to attend you to take the oath required by the Constitution. It will be administered by the Chancellor of the State of New York."

Washington stood, gave a short bow to Adams and said simply, "I am ready to proceed."

Washington took the oath of office on a portico of Federal Hall that overlooked Wall Street and Broad Street. It was a covered balcony of some 480 square feet with three doors at the rear, a window at either end, and an iron railing across the open side.

When Washington stepped through the center door to the railing, a roar went up from the

Washington takes the oath of office on the portico of Federal Hall in New York.

hundreds of upturned faces in the streets be-
low and from the rooftops and windows facing
Federal Hall.

Touched, he put his right hand on his heart
and bowed repeatedly to right and left. This

simple gesture, intended only to acknowledge his welcome, intensified the acclaim.

Finally, Washington pulled back and sat in an armchair as members of Congress crowded onto the portico, and the Chancellor of New York, Robert R. Livingston, prepared to administer the oath.

When all seemed ready, Washington rose and moved close to the balcony, his right side to the street. Livingston, who had been a member of Congress when Washington was appointed commander in chief in 1776, faced him a few feet away, his left side to the street.

Between them, facing the street, stood Samuel Otis, secretary of the Senate. Otis held a small red cushion in his hands. Atop the cushion rested a large leather Bible.

When Otis lifted the Bible, Washington immediately placed his right hand on it, palm down. At that moment, it was so quiet that Washington, Otis, and Livingston could have been alone.

"Do you solemnly swear," asked Livingston, breaking the silence, "that you will faithfully execute the office of President of the United States and will, to the best of your ability, preserve, protect, and defend the Constitution of the United States?"

In a low voice tinged with emotion, Washington responded:

"I solemnly swear that I will faithfully execute the office of the President of the United States and will, to the best of my ability, preserve, protect, and defend the Constitution of the United States."

Then he added, "So help me God." At the last word, he quickly bent forward and kissed the Bible.

"It is done!" cried Livingston, his hands pumping skyward.

The crowds outside Federal Hall applauded and cheered wildly as a cacophony of cannon shots, horns, and whistles erupted in the harbor. Suddenly, however, a hush fell over those in the immediate area of the Hall. A fluttering object sliding slowly but smoothly upward above the building's cupola drew every eye. It was the American flag.

Book Three

Minutes after being sworn into office as the first president of the United States on April 30, 1789, George Washington rose from his seat on the dais of the Senate chamber inside New York's Federal Hall to address the newly elected members of the Senate and the House of Representatives. As Washington spoke, there were no grand gestures, no poses, no ringing phrases, no bombast, and no promises.

Unmistakably, however, there was emotion. While suppressed, it was clearly evident in his voice; a low, tremulous baritone that barely reached the far corners of the ornate, rectangular room.

And while Washington's large body—erect as always—was fairly still, emotion could also be detected in his big hands, for they shook slightly as they repeatedly changed places, one holding a manuscript, while the fingers of the other were stuffed into a pocket of his plain, brown, proudly worn, American-made suit.

Like so much of what had already taken place and would soon follow, Washington's inaugural speech was a first for the new nation. Grave, humble, considerate, and brief, it was also unlike any other inaugural address that would follow over the course of more than two centuries.

"Fellow citizens of the Senate and the House of Representatives," he began slowly. "Among the vicissitudes incident to life, no event could have filled me with greater anxieties than that of which was transmitted by your order and received on the fourteenth day of the present month."

On the one hand, he said, he was "summoned by my country, whose voice I can never hear but with veneration and love" from a retirement that was "dear to me." On the other hand, he was overwhelmed by the "magnitude and difficulty of the trust to which the voice of my country called me."

After remarking that he had inherited "inferior endowments from nature" and was "unpracticed in the duties of civil administration," he said: "It would be peculiarly improper to omit in this first official act my fervent supplications to the Almighty Being who rules over the Universe, who presides in the Councils of Nations and whose providential aids can [correct] every human defect."

He noted that the Constitution required the president "to recommend to your consideration such measures he shall judge necessary and expedient" to the operation of the government. He said, however, he would defer such action to Congress.

He did so, he added, because he was sure that "no local prejudices or attachments, no separate views nor party animosities" would "misdirect the comprehensive and equal eye" of that body.

He then asked Congress to decide whether there should be amendments added to the Constitution, as many officials had advocated during the stormy ratification process.

In closing, he said: "Having thus imparted to you my sentiments, as they have been awakened by the occasion which brings us together, I shall take my present leave; but not without resorting once more to the benign parent of the human race, in humble supplication that since he has been pleased to favor the American people with opportunities for deliberating, in perfect tranquility and dispositions, for deciding with unparalleled unanimity on a form of government for the security of their union and the advancement of their happiness."

Washington's audience was deeply moved, not so much by what was said, as by the memories he evoked, his sincerity, expressions of humility, and earnestness.

As one senator was to say later, "It was a very touching scene and quite of the solemn kind. It produced emotions of the most affecting kind upon the members. I sat entranced."

A minister from France who witnessed the inauguration wrote to his government, "Never has a sovereign reigned more completely in the hearts of his subjects. He has the soul, look and figure of a hero united in him."

Another witness reported that virtually every member wept openly as Washington spoke.

Washington's demeanor and the reaction of his audience that fateful day are understandable. The United States, after all, had fought a long, bloody war against overwhelming odds to achieve independence from one of the most powerful nations on earth.

And now, for the first time in the history of the world, this new country had launched an effort to demonstrate that ordinary people, rich and poor, could govern themselves.

After his address, Washington led the Congressmen and guests from Federal Hall to nearby St. Paul's Chapel to hear a "divine service" to be given by the "Chaplain of Congress."

As the group, in a column of twos, slowly took the seven-hundred-yard walk through cheering crowds, two questions surely must have nagged at many minds: Could America's bold experiment in the science of government succeed? And if it didn't, what would happen to the country?

From the very first day he took office, the new president had to carefully gauge and weigh his every step, action, and public utterance.

There were no guidelines. No established institutions. No precedents. And no pattern of behavior to follow. "I walk on untrodden ground," he said.

As he struggled to get his untried government moving, he faced literally hundreds of difficult problems. Among the more serious:

• Ignoring the terms of its peace treaty with the United States, Britain continued to occupy military posts in U.S. territory in the Northwest, which included much of what is now Ohio. In addition, the British were encouraging Indian tribes to attack American settlers on the frontier.

• In the southwest portion of the country, then land claimed by Georgia, Spain blocked American navigation on the Mississippi River and, like the English, encouraged the Indians to halt westward expansion.

• The country was severely in debt, and inflation cheapened the value of its money every day.

• The seat of government had yet to be fully established.

• Imperfections in the Constitution had to be corrected.

• A judicial system had to be created.

• Laws and treaties had to be written and executed.

• The legislative, judicial, and executive branches of the government had to be staffed, established in a permanent location, and organized so they could begin operation.

• The nation was without a navy, and the army had dwindled to fewer than eight hundred men.

• Pirates in the Mediterranean Sea were attacking and seizing American ships.

Before addressing any of these difficulties, however, Washington was forced to tackle a problem that created an immediate crisis in the spring of 1789: etiquette.

"The President of the United States wishes to avail himself of your sentiments on the following points . . ."

So began a memo dated May 10, 1789, addressed to Vice President John Adams, Congressman James Madison, and John Jay and Alexander Hamilton, members of the now defunct Congress that had existed under the Articles of Confederation.

Washington wanted to know the following: How should he spend his waking hours?

In the first ten days of his term in office, his life had been in chaos. He was deluged with invitations to all sorts of social affairs—afternoon teas, dances, theater and musical performances, and an endless list of dinners.

Worse yet, scores of uninvited visitors appeared at his door at all hours of the day and night. Some hoped to conduct business. Some came to gawk, and perhaps shake the president's hand. Others fully expected to join him for dinner!

"I am faced with a horrendous, but delicate problem," Washington wrote to Martha, who was still at Mount Vernon awaiting a call to join him in New York.

"On the one hand, I must have time to do my work, which is extensive," he added. "On the other, I cannot remain secluded, and I must not offend important members of the Government or the public."

In his letter to Adams, Hamilton, Jay, and Madison, Washington posed nine questions:

1. Should his line of conduct be "equally distant" from all kinds of company and totally secluded from society? If so, how was it to be done?

2. What would be the "least exceptionable method" to introduce a social and business schedule?

3. Would one day a week be "sufficient for receiving visits of compliment?"

4. Would it "tend to prompt impertinent applications and involve disagreeable consequences" to let people know that the president would "give audiences to persons who may have business" with him at eight o'clock every morning?

5. Could he invite small groups of government officials to dine with him on days scheduled for that purpose "without exciting clamors in the rest of the Community?"

6. Would it be "satisfactory to the public" to have "entertainments" on the anniversaries of the Declaration of

Independence, the colonies' alliance with France during the Revolution, peace with Great Britain, and the signing of the Constitution?

7. Would there be any "impropriety" in making strictly informal visits to friends and members of the public for purely social purposes? And would people be offended if he were to "rarely" appear at tea parties?

8. When Congress was in recess, should he tour various parts of the country to become "better acquainted with their principal characters and internal circumstances as well as to be more accessible to numbers of well-informed persons" who might give him useful information "and advice on political subjects"?

9. Whatever arrangements were made for the use of the president's time, should Congress cover the expense of such activities?

Washington noted it would be much easier to "commence the administration" on a "sound system" than to "correct errors" after they were "confirmed by habit." He believed, he said, that in "all matters of business and etiquette" he should maintain "the dignity of office," but not give the impression he was haughty or unnecessarily reserved.

All four of those who received Washington's letter answered differently. Washington himself finally decided:

• He would hold two receptions a week; one for men only, every Tuesday from three to four. The other would be a tea party hosted by Martha for men and women, to be held Friday evenings.

• He would accept no invitations.

• He would occasionally attend a theater performance and visit a local farm.

• He would wait until Martha arrived before making any further social plans.

Had he not taken this step, he said later, he would have been "unable to attend any sort of business" unless he did so when it was normally time to eat and sleep.

How should Washington be addressed or announced when he appeared in public? For days, the House and Senate couldn't agree.

A committee of the Senate, led by John Adams, thought the head of the executive branch of the new government should be called: "His Most Benign Highness the President of the United States."

Another senate committee thought Washington should be addressed as "His Highness the President of the United States of America and Protector of the Rights of same." The House objected. The proper title for Washington should be simply and plainly: "the President of the United States," as called for in the Constitution.

On May 14, two weeks after Washington took office, the House won this touchy first battle with the Senate.

One senator who agreed with the House was William Maclay, Washington's harshest critic. He said while he had "no clue" about Washington's feelings on the matter, he suspected the president had dropped a hint to "his confidants" suggesting a royal title.

"No matter," Maclay said. "I have, by plowing with the [cattle] in the other House, completely defeated" the proposal put forth by the Senate.

One newspaper had a different view. "Let us lisp nothing but the pure names of men," the *Boston Centinel* said. "Plain John Anybody should be our address. 'Mr.' signifies 'Master' and leads to slavery; therefore away with it."

A few days later, Congressman Joseph Jones wrote Madison saying that he was "pleased with the plain manly style of address, 'George Washington, President.' The present name wants no titles to grace it, and should the office be filled by an unworthy person, the style will not dignify the man, or cast a beam of light around his head." With that weighty issue settled, Congress turned its attention to other matters.

Under the Articles of Confederation—introduced in 1776 during the war with Britain—Congress was a single body with virtually no power. It did, however, organize and establish four departments: Foreign Affairs, War, Post Office, and Treasury,

Washington was no stranger to the way government usually operated. He had, after all, been a member of the Virginia House of Burgesses for several years, served in the Continental Congress of 1774 and 1775 and, as commander in chief of the Continental Army for almost nine years, had dealt frequently with Congress and the thirteen state governments.

The Constitution, however, created something new and puzzling: a system of "checks and balances" among the legislative, judicial, and executive branches of government. The idea behind this system was to prevent any one branch from dominating the others. But it raised a question that confounded many: What powers did the Constitution give each branch? As the "chief executive," Washington was determined to find the answer and make the system work.

The role was unofficial, its duties undefined and intangible. Still, the post of "First Lady," introduced by Martha Washington, was and remains a unique and important position in presidential politics.

That this small, modest, unassuming, fifty-seven-year-old woman would be an asset to President Washington became evident the moment she left Mount Vernon on May 16, 1788, to join her husband in faraway New York.

With her in the family's sparkling yellow four-horse carriage were two of her four grandchildren, Eleanor "Nelly" Custis, age ten, and George "Little Washington" Parke Custis, age nine. Riding as an escort was Robert Lewis, a nephew of the president.

All along the route of her eleven-day journey, Martha was feted and honored by an adoring public. On her arrival in Baltimore, for example, she was treated to a huge display of

Martha Washington, the first First Lady (left), entertains at the "president's house" in New York.

fireworks, followed by a party and a musical serenade that lasted until two in the morning.

Three hours after it ended, Martha was on her way. Some ten miles from Philadelphia, the next stop on her journey, she was greeted by local dignitaries and two troops of Light Horse.

Later, more than a hundred of the town's leading citizens led her carriage through cheering crowds that clogged the streets of Philadelphia. As the procession moved along, cannons boomed a thirteen-gun salute, and every church bell pealed a welcome.

Clearly, the public remembered that Martha Washington, at the risk of her life and health, had joined her husband at the army's winter quarters no fewer than six times during the Revolution.

The *Pennsylvania Packet* seemed to speak for all when it said: "The present occasion recalled the remembrance of those interesting scenes, in which, by her presence, she contributed to relieve the cares of our beloved Chief, and to soothe the anxious moments of his military concerns—gratitude marked the recollection, and every countenance bespoke the feelings of an affectionate respect."

While crossing the Hudson River from New Jersey to New York, Martha was again saluted by thirteen cannon shots. And at the dock to meet her was the governor of New York, George

Clinton, more dignitaries, and a huge, applauding crowd.

Once the children were in school and she was settled in the three-story "President's House" on Pearl and Cherry streets, Martha turned her attention toward her new duties. It was then that she began to emerge as America's first First Lady.

During her thirty-year marriage to George Washington, Martha was often overshadowed by her husband's fame and position. In her new role as the wife of the president, however, she shone. One of her admirers was sharp-tongued Abigail Adams, wife of the vice president.

"I took the earliest opportunity to go and pay my respects to Mrs. Washington," Mrs. Adams wrote in a letter to her sister. "She received me with great ease and politeness. She is plain in her dress, but that plainness is the best of every article. Her hair is white, her teeth beautiful."

"Her manners are modest and unassuming, dignified and feminine, not the tincture of hauteur about her," she added.

Abigail Adams, who was with her husband when he served as ambassador to Great Britain, had been exposed to royalty and became something of a social critic. In a second letter, she said: "Mrs. Washington is one of those unassuming characters which create love and esteem. A most becoming pleasantness sits upon her countenance and an unaffected deportment which renders her the object of veneration and respect. With all these feelings and sensations, I found myself much more deeply impressed than I ever did before their Majesties of Britain."

Martha, however, had no illusions about her new role in life. "I would much rather be at home than in a place where a great many younger and gayer women would be prodigiously pleased," she wrote a friend after her arrival in New York. "I know too much of the vanity of human affairs to expect felicity from the splendid scenes of public life," she added. "I am still determined to be cheerful and to be happy in whatever situation I may be; for I have also learned from experience that the greater part of our happiness or misery depends upon our dispositions, and not upon our circumstances."

Martha was hostess of the president's dinner parties and receptions. Each Friday evening, however, she invited groups of local citizens and members of Congress to a reception of her own. The invitations were eagerly sought after and highly prized.

Arriving in their finest clothing and jewelry and newest hairdos, the female guests and their escorts were announced as they entered the receiving room. They were then led to Martha's chair, introduced, and seated apart from her. After a greeting from the president, the guests were escorted into a second room, where they could circulate and visit freely and sample the refreshments.

Occasionally, a woman would mistakenly sit in the chair to Martha's right, which was reserved for the wife of the vice president. Whenever this occurred, Washington, with extreme politeness, would correct matters.

As Abigail noted, "This same president has so happy a faculty of appearing to accommodate and yet carrying his point, that if he was not really one of the best-intentioned men in the world, he might be a very dangerous one.

"He is polite with dignity, affable without familiarity, distant without haughtiness, grave without austerity, modest, wise and good," Abigail said.

She added that Washington had so much grace, ease, and dignity, he "leaves Royal [King] George far behind him."

In the middle of June 1788, however, receptions and parties at the President's House were suddenly suspended. The president was seriously ill.

Rumors that Washington was dying swept through the city like wildfire. When Doctor Samuel Bard examined the president, he discovered a life-threatening tumor on Washington's left thigh.

"The tumor must be removed as soon as possible," the doctor said.

"Then remove it," Washington answered, knowing that there was no medication in existence that would ease the pain of surgery.

Digging deep with his scalpel, Dr. Bard successfully excised the tumor.

Under Martha's soothing hands, Washington began a slow, painful recovery. He was, however, strongly motivated to get back on his feet: The New York state militia and the State Society of the Cincinnati, an organization formed by the retired officers of the Continental Army, planned to honor him on Independence Day.

"I must be ready," he told Martha, as he grimly stuck to a regimen of daily exercises.

When the day came, he stood at attention in the doorway of his house dressed in his wartime uniform, Martha at his side. Up the street came the militia with its band, cheered on by a great crowd.

After the parade passed, General Baron Friedrich von Steuben, president of the Cincinnati and Washington's drill master in the Revolution, stood before the Washingtons with a band of proud uniformed members.

"The Society of the Cincinnati of the State of New York have instructed this delegation to present to you, sir, their sentiments of the profoundest respect," Von Steuben said. "In common with all good citizens of the United States of America, they join together in their ardent wishes for the preservation of your life, health and prospects.

"Under your conduct, sir, this band of soldiers was led to glory and to conquest, and we feel confident that under your administration our country will speedily arrive at an enviable state of prosperity and happiness," von Steuben added.

It was a prophetic statement, for that day Washington signed his first major bill for "laying a duty on goods, wares and merchandising imported into the United States."

On the fourth of July, 1776, Americans had declared their spiritual and political independence. Now, thirteen years later, the nation finally declared its fiscal independence, making it clear that the government of "We the people" was in motion.

$\mathcal{A}$lmost from the day he took office, Washington was confronted with a nightmarish problem he had never faced in all his years of public service: job seekers.

His small office in the president's house was flooded with some three thousand applications for placements that ranged from clerks to judges to diplomats. And those who had access to Washington, officially and unofficially, pleaded for the employment of many more.

Despite often angry, lengthy debates and frayed nerves, openings in the government evolved rather quickly as Congress established the Departments of War, State, and the Treasury.

Washington began the difficult, time-consuming chore of building the executive branch by nominating his former Chief of Artillery, Henry Knox, as secretary of war, Alexander Hamilton as secretary of the Treasury, and Thomas Jefferson as secretary of state. He also nominated John Jay as chief justice of the Supreme Court and Edmund Randolph as attorney general. All of these nominations easily won the approval of the Senate.

The hectic labor in this first session of Congress was not limited to personnel matters, however. There were also these developments:

Washington's first Cabinet included (from left to right) Henry Knox as secretary of war, Thomas Jefferson as secretary of state, Edmund Randolph (with back turned) as attorney general, and Alexander Hamilton as secretary of the Treasury. Washington is standing at the right.

• Although he had agreed to serve at his own expense (just as he had during the war), Washington's salary was fixed at $25,000 a year and Vice President Adams's at $5,000.

• Twelve amendments to the Constitution were recommended. Eventually, ten were adopted as the Bill of Rights.

• The federal courts were established.

For Washington, much of this intensive activity created a continuous and persistent need to communicate with both houses of Congress.

In conferring with his "cabinet" about this problem, Washington said, "We must be careful to establish a correct and workable precedent when communicating with the other bodies."

As stipulated by the Constitution, Washington was to seek the "advice and consent" of the Senate on such subjects as treaties. But how was this to be done? Should he go to the Senate in person, or send a secretary? Or should he communicate in writing?

In midsummer, Washington decided to ask for the Senate's advice and consent on a treaty and a set of instructions he wanted to forward as quickly as possible to a three-man commission poised to meet with the powerful Creek Indians. He decided to do it in person.

On entering the Senate chamber with Secretary of War Henry Knox at his side, Washington took the chair as Vice President John Adams, normally the presiding officer, moved to a seat among the senators.

After reading aloud the first part of the proposed instructions and the treaty Washington had brought with him, Adams asked for the Senate's "advice and consent" as required by the Constitution.

The senators hemmed and hawed, then asked Adams to read the material again. He did. And again he asked for "advice and consent."

Senator William Maclay objected. "This business is new to the Senate," he argued. "We know it is important. But it is our duty to inform ourselves."

There was more discussion. More delay. Suddenly, a motion was made to refer the matter to a committee "for study."

Exasperated, Washington jumped to his feet. "You have all the information you need. If you are not willing to give your advice and consent, it defeats every purpose of my coming here!"

It was then suggested the matter be postponed until a later date. His anger subsiding, Washington reluctantly agreed.

When he took time out of his busy schedule for a reappearance, however, the Senate spent even more time haggling over the language of the treaty. When the debate ended, only a few words had been changed.

On leaving the chamber, a fuming Washington muttered, "I'll be damned if I'll ever come here again for 'advice and consent.'"

He never did. Neither has any other president since.

As always, Washington's duties were often interrupted by personal matters. In August, his sister, Betty Lewis, sent him news he had long expected: Their mother, Mary Ball Washington, was gravely ill.

"God only knows how it will end; I dread the consequence," his sister wrote from Fredericksburg, Virginia. "She is sensible of it and is perfectly resigned. She wishes to hear from you; she will not believe you are well till she has it from your hand."

Long a victim of breast cancer, Mrs. Washington died on August 25, 1789. She was eighty-one, an age few men or women ever reached in her generation.

In some ways, Washington and his mother were a lot alike. Physically, for example, both were tall, strong, and sturdy. Temperamentally, they both were strong-willed and determined. Both loved and admired nature. Their relationship, however, was often strained.

Washington's father died when George was eleven, leaving behind five children on a poor, run-down farm on the banks of the Rappahannock River near Fredericksburg. As the oldest child, George was expected to help his mother take care of his siblings and work the farm.

But George had other ideas. When he grew up, he wanted to be like his half-brother, Lawrence. Lawrence owned a plantation on the Potomac River. He had married Anne Fairfax, the daughter of one of the wealthiest men in Virginia. He was commander of the Virginia militia and had successful business connections in high places.

As he grew into his teens, Washington tried to leave the farm and join the British Navy. In the first of several attempts to keep her son at home, his mother agreed to let him go, then changed her mind.

While Washington dutifully called on his mother whenever he could, his visits were brief. That they loved each other, however, there is no doubt.

At the news of her death, Washington temporarily suspended all receptions and public appearances. He also followed a practice established by the Continental Congress in 1774, which limited the mourning dress of members to "black crepe or ribbon on the arm or hat, for gentlemen, and a black ribbon and necklace for ladies."

For the men at the President's House, Washington also ordered black cockades, sword knots, and arm bands.

In a letter to Betty, he said, "Awful and affecting as the death of a parent is, there is consolation in knowing that Heaven has spared ours to an age beyond which few attain, and favored her with the full employment of her mental faculties and as much bodily strength as usually falls to the lot of fourscore [four times twenty].

"Under these considerations and a hope that she is translated to a happier place, it is the duty of her relatives to yield due submission to the decrees of the creator.

"When I was last in Fredericksburg, I took a final leave of my Mother, never expecting to see her more."

When Congress adjourned for the first time in late September 1789, the government created by the Constitution only two years earlier was up and running.

In a letter to a British historian, Washington noted that the new government was "completely organized and in operation."

"We have greater reason than the most sanguine could expect to be satisfied with its success," he added. "Opposition to the government is either no more or hides its head."

He also noted that North Carolina had finally joined the ranks of the new government and that Rhode Island would soon follow.

Actually, however, there was a long list of problems that needed to be solved before the United States could emerge as a fully functioning, strong, and independent nation. Among them were these:

• Spain had yet to relinquish control of the Mississippi.

• England still retained its military posts in the northwest.

• There was no commercial treaty between England and the United States.

• Trade with the West Indies had not been stabilized.

• Relations with Indians in the northwest and southwest were in a dangerous state.

The most serious and vexing problem of all, however, was the matter of communicating with the public. It was a problem Washington recognized almost immediately after taking office.

When the United States was born, the only way people could communicate effectively was by writing letters, speaking face to face, or through pamphlet-sized newspapers.

To lead the nation with a sure hand, Washington knew he must have first-hand information about what was going on beyond New York.

"I must learn more about manufacturing, commerce, farming, and any activity that leads to growth and expansion," he explained to Martha. "And I need to know how people are reacting to their new government."

Washington also thought that more citizens should have the opportunity to see and hear the man they had elected as president. After all, only a tiny fraction of the population knew what he looked like, or had ever heard him speak. As a result, Washington made a trip through New England two weeks after Congress adjourned. Traveling mostly by coach, he was accompanied by two aides, Tobias Lear and William Jackson, and six servants.

He noted in his diary that the towns and farms he passed through were very close together and separated by stone fences, "which are indeed easily made as the country is immensely stony."

Along the way, he talked to local farmers and learned that they had a good crop of rye and wheat that year even though they had "sown rather sparingly" because seeds were usually destroyed "by what is called the Hessian fly."

Passing through Norwalk and Fairfield, Connecticut, he saw the still-standing chimneys of many burnt-out houses, "the destructive evidences of British cruelty."

"The principal export from Norwalk & Fairfield is horses and cattle—salted beef & pork, lumber & Indian corn, to the West Indies—and in small degree wheat & flour," he wrote in his diary.

New Haven was a city of some "4,000 souls," an Episcopal church, three meeting houses, and a college called Yale that had "120 students under the auspices of Doctor Styles."

"The linnen manufacture of this place does not appear to be of so much importance as I had been led to believe," he wrote.

In Wallingford, which he reached on the 19th, he saw the "white mulberry growing, raised from the seed to feed the silkworm," his diary continues. "We also saw samples of lustring which has been manufactured from the cocoon raised in this town, and silk thread very fine. This, except the weaving, is the work of private families without interference with other business, and is likely to turn out a beneficial amusement."

Wherever he went, Washington was greeted and feted by enthusiastic local officials and citizens. In Boston, however, he ran into an embarrassing political storm.

Who was more important, the governor of a state, or the president of the United States?

This sticky question cropped up when Massachusetts Governor John Hancock—a well-known advocate of state supremacy—invited Washington to dine with him. Washington accepted the invitation.

When the president arrived in Boston, however, Hancock sent word that he was too ill to journey to the tavern where Washington was staying. Washington, he said, should come to his house for dinner.

Washington, according to his diary, "excused myself" and had dinner "in my lodgings, where the Vice President [John Adams] favoured me with his company."

The next evening, Lieutenant Governor Samuel Adams and two members of the Governor's Council called on Washington to "express the Governor's concern."

"I informed them in explicit terms that I should not see the Governor unless it was at my own lodgings," Washington's diary noted.

Swathed in bandages and full of apology, Hancock arrived at the president's tavern the next day to pay his respects. That settled this question of protocol for all time.

On leaving Boston, Washington visited a manufacturer of sailcloth.

"They have manufactured 32 pieces of duck of 30 or 40 yards each in a week," he wrote in his diary. "They have 28 looms at work & 14 girls spinning with both hands (the flax being fastened to their waist). Children (girls) turn the wheels for them, and with this assistance each spinner can turn out 14 pounds of thread per day when they stick to it, but as they are paid by the piece, or work they do, there is no other restraint upon them but to come at 8 o'clock in the morning and return (home) at 6 in the evening. They are daughters of [impoverished] families, and are girls of Character—none others are admitted."

He also made these observations during the remainder of his twenty-nine-day trip:

• At Harvard College he was amazed to find a library that contained 13,000 volumes and a "curious piece of mechanism for showing the revolutions of the Sun, Earth, and many other of the planets."

• In Marblehead, Massachusetts, he found "5,000 souls" living in a town that "has the appearance of antiquity; the houses are old, the streets dirty—and the common people not very clean." The "chief employment," he said, was fishing. "About 800 men and boys are engaged in this business" working aboard 110 vessels.

• The trip from Watertown to Needham was pleasant, but, he said, the "roads in every part of this state are amazingly crooked" to suit the convenience of every man's field. Forced to skirt a farmer's cultivated fields, travelers often had to ride many extra miles to get from one town to another. "And the directions you receive from people are equally blind and ignorant," Washington complained.

During his tour, Washington avoided Rhode Island, which had not yet ratified the Constitution. He arrived back in New York on Friday, November 13, just in time for one of Martha's parties. From that day on, however, Washington's tenure in office became increasingly difficult.

George Washington often made it clear that he was opposed to titles that smacked of royalty. He liked pomp and ceremony, however, believing that it added to the dignity and luster of his office.

So it's not surprising that he carefully planned virtually every detail of the short ride from the President's House to City Hall on January 8, 1790. For that was the day he was to address the nation and Congress before the start of its second session.

When Washington left his home at precisely 11 A.M., two aides in military uniforms, Colonel David Humphreys and Major William Jackson, led the way mounted on white horses. The Washingtons were immediately behind in the family coach, which was pulled by six cream-colored horses with neatly groomed manes and tails.

Following the President in another carriage were his two personal secretaries, Tobias Lear and Thomas Nelson Jr. Next came Washington's nephew, Robert Lewis, who was riding yet another white horse. Strung out behind Lewis were carriages carrying the chief justice of the United States and the secretaries of War and Treasury and their wives.

As might be expected, the parade of dignitaries brought out a huge, cheering crowd, which clearly justified Washington's efforts.

In a brief message, Washington called for an improvement in the nation's defenses, saying, "being prepared for war is one of the most effectual means of preserving peace."

The first official residence for the president of the United States was a mansion on Pearl and Cherry streets in New York.

He also urged Congress to:
• Provide for more protection of the western frontier.
• Establish naturalization laws.
• Establish a system of uniform weights and measurements.
• Expand the postal service.
• Promote science and literature.
• Establish regulations covering patents.
• Take a census.

• Help institutions of learning in general and establish a national university, pointing out that "knowledge is in every country the surest basis of public happiness."

As he spoke, many wondered where the money would come from to support all these projects and, at the same time, pay the nation's enormous debt, estimated at a then-staggering seventy-five million dollars.

The answer came a week later in a proposal Washington sent to the House of Representatives without comment. The proposal was written by the secretary of the Treasury, Alexander Hamilton.

Alexander Hamilton was born to poor, unmarried parents in the British West Indies on January 11, 1757. His father, James Hamilton, a worthless son of a prominent Scottish family, left their home in St. Croix when Alexander was ten. And Rachel, his destitute mother, died when he was eleven.

As a teenager, Hamilton was described as "under middle size, thin in person" and "rather frail." All who knew him agreed that he was handsome, however, with dark blue, deep-set eyes, reddish-brown hair, and rosy cheeks.

By the time he was sixteen, he was keeping the books for Nicholas Cruger, the owner of an export-import house. And he was writing letters on behalf of Cruger's firm to planters, sea captains, and government officials all over the West Indies and even along the coast of the United States.

With Cruger's help, young Hamilton left the West Indies for the United States in 1773. Not long after his arrival in New York, Alexander enrolled at tiny King's College (now Columbia University). An exceptionally good student, he studied hard and advanced rapidly. He also became quite skilled at writing and debating.

When the Revolutionary War broke out, Hamilton joined the New York militia and became captain of an artillery unit. He met Washington as the army was retreating from New York in the fall of 1776. Six months later, at age twenty, he became an aide to Washington, a post he held for four years.

Hamilton remained with the army until the British defeat at Yorktown. He then became active in New York politics, studied law, speedily passed his bar examinations, and set up a lucrative law practice. During 1787 and 1788, he had played a key role in New York's adoption of the Constitution.

On September 11, 1789, Hamilton was named secretary of the Treasury, Washington's first appointee. Four months later, Hamilton introduced a plan to free the nation from debt; a plan so controversial it nearly wrecked Washington's administration. It also changed the face of politics in the United States forever.

Unquestionably, Washington was the head of the new government. But one department—and only one—had a direct link to Congress: Treasury.

As secretary of the Treasury, Alexander Hamilton was required by the Constitution to "make reports and give information to either branch of the legislature, in person or in writing respecting all matters referred to him by the Senate or the House of Representatives."

In early October 1789, the House asked Hamilton for a "Report on the Public Credit" in writing. Three months later, the House got what it asked for: a 15,000-word report, plus 20,000 words of appendixes and proposed laws.

His plan, Hamilton said, contained the following "plain and undeniable truths":

• That emergencies occur "in the affairs of nations" making it necessary to borrow money.

• That loans in times of danger, "especially from foreign war," are an indispensable resource "even to the wealthiest" nations.

• In a country with little capital, like the United States, the need to obtain loans as a resource during emergencies was "urgent."

• Since the need to borrow money "cannot be doubted," the credit of a nation must be well established if money is to be obtained on good terms.

Hamilton said that there was only one way the country could maintain a good credit rating: "By good faith. By a punctual performance of its contracts. States, like individuals, who observe their [payments] are respected and trusted, while the reverse is the fate of those who pursue an opposite conduct."

According to Hamilton's figures, however, the United States owed fifty-four million dollars, of which fifteen million dollars was unpaid interest!

The House members were stunned. How, they wondered, could the United States overcome so much debt and establish credit when the treasury was empty, and there was no method in place to raise money?

Before the readers of Hamilton's report came to the answer, they were staggered by another proposal: The federal government, Hamilton said, should assume the wartime debts of the states—another twenty-one million dollars!

This was only fair, Hamilton explained, because the states originally assumed the debt, most of it in certificates to soldiers, farmers, and small businessmen, during the war to save the union; and since the union had survived, it should take over the states' debts.

Simply put, the main objective of Hamilton's plan was to reduce the interest on all debt, and pay off the money originally borrowed at the rate of two per cent a year. To accomplish this, Hamilton proposed to raise money through the sale of bonds, which would be funded by the collection of taxes; increase duties on imported wines, liquors, tea, and coffee; impose excise taxes on alcoholic spirits produced in the United States; and use the profits from the Post Office to help make payments on debts.

Washington approved the plan and sent it forward without comment. He knew, however, that it would provoke a battle. He was right.

 "It's unfair and unjust!"

So cried Virginia Representative James Madison shortly after Alexander Hamilton presented his complicated plan to solve the nation's financial crisis.

Congress was shocked by this uncharacteristic outburst. After all, Madison and Hamilton had for years been among Washington's staunchest supporters. And, following Washington's lead, both had fought hard to establish the Constitution and to create a strong central government.

Hamilton's monetary plan, however, infuriated Madison, especially the proposal for honoring government certificates of credit. Instead of hard currency, these certificates were given to soldiers during the Revolution in lieu of pay and to farmers and small businessmen in exchange for food and goods supplied the army. As time went on, the holders of such certificates, desperate for cash, sold them to speculators for as little as ten cents on the dollar.

Under Hamilton's plan, the certificates would be worth their full face value. To Madison, this meant the holders of purchased certificates would get rich while the original owners would get nothing. The "original sufferers" should get some of the value of the certificates when redeemed by the present owners, Madison argued.

"A debt was fairly contracted," he pointed out. "According to justice and good faith, it ought to have been paid in gold or silver. A piece of paper only was substituted. Was this paper equal in value to gold or silver? No. It was worth no more than one-eighth or one-seventh of that value. Was this depreciated paper freely accepted? No. The government offered that or nothing."

Hamilton and the supporters of his plan objected vigorously to Madison's proposal. Each certificate, they argued, clearly stated the amount owed was to be paid to "the bearer," or present owner. They also insisted it would be impossible and extremely expensive to track down all the original owners of certificates.

Madison's "discrimination" plan was voted down by a large majority. But Madison wasn't finished; he now launched a debate over the "assumption" of state debts.

This part of the plan meant some states would profit over others. If the central government was going to pay the existing debts of delinquent states, Madison insisted, it should reimburse those states, such as Virginia, that had paid their war debt.

As members of Congress wrangled over the "assumption" issue early in 1790, it became entangled with another bill aimed at establishing a permanent home for the new government.

As the arguments over these two bills continued to escalate, an important new character left the wings and reluctantly stepped into the political arena. His name was Thomas Jefferson.

After five-and-a-half years as the American minister to France, Thomas Jefferson was granted a leave of absence to return home.

On his arrival in Norfolk, Virginia, in December 1789, after a fifty-eight-day journey (twenty-nine of them spent at sea), the forty-seven-year-old Virginia aristocrat received a letter from Washington dated October 13. The lanky redhead had been nominated to the new office of secretary of state.

Jefferson's reply was ambivalent. He began his response by saying that after taking care of his personal affairs, which included a wedding for his daughter, Martha, he would rather go back to his old post in Europe.

The nomination, he said, "may end disagreeably for me with the criticisms and censures of the public, just indeed in their intentions, but sometimes misinformed and misled."

Jefferson said, however, that he would accept the nomination if Washington insisted. He closed by adding, "My chief comfort will be to work under your eye, my only shelter the authority of your name, and the wisdom of measures dictated by you and implicitly executed by me."

Thomas Jefferson accepted his appointment as the first secretary of state reluctantly.

On March 21, Washington noted in his diary: "Received Mr. Jefferson, Minister of State, at about one o'clock."

For weeks, Congress fought over Hamilton's "assumption" bill and the bill to "establish the permanent seat of the Government of the United States."

Representatives of the agricultural states, mainly in the South, said Hamilton's highly complex funding plan favored the rich over the poor; the speculator over the war veteran and the farmer.

The northern interests, however, insisted that Hamilton's plan was the only way the country could be put on a sound financial footing and achieve prosperity.

On April 12, the assumption bill was tested in a roll-call vote. It lost by two votes.

The bill to locate the nation's permanent capital aggravated the situation. New Yorkers wanted it in New York, Pennsylvanians in Philadelphia. The Southerners insisted, however, that the capital should be as far away from the "corrupting influence" of the financial centers—New York and Philadelphia—as possible.

Virginians favored the banks of the Potomac, pointing out that the capital would be centrally located; 1,240 miles from the nation's northernmost point and 1,270 miles from its southernmost boundary.

As the battle raged on, Washington came down with pneumonia. On May 15, the fifth day of his illness, two of the three physicians attending the president believed he was "in the act of death."

"You cannot conceive of the public alarm on this occasion," Jefferson was to write. "It proves how much depends on his life."

By four o'clock on the 15th, however, Washington passed the crisis and began to improve rapidly. In a week, he was able to leave the house.

And while he put on a cheerful face for Martha's benefit, he wrote a friend, "I have already had within less than a year, two severe attacks, the last worse than the first. A third more than probable will put me to sleep with my fathers."

In another letter, he said his doctors told him to get more exercise and not work so hard. "I cannot, however, avoid persuading myself that it is essential to accomplish whatever I have undertaken (though reluctantly) to the best of my abilities," he added.

He went on to say he was pleased by the performance of the various members of his Cabinet. "I feel myself supported by able coadjutors who harmonize extremely well together."

Two of Washington's "coadjutors" soon teamed up to solve the twin problems threatening to tear his administration—and the country—apart. That, however, was the end of any attempt to "harmonize."

On a warm spring day in 1790, Thomas Jefferson had a chance meeting with Alexander Hamilton in front of Washington's second home in New York, which was located on Broadway near Trinity Church.

The secretary of state was startled to observe that Hamilton was not his usual dapper self. "He was," as Jefferson put it later, "sober, haggard, and dejected beyond description, even his dress uncouth and neglected."

When Jefferson asked what was wrong, Hamilton answered worriedly, "The assumption bill has been voted down five times. It must pass or our financial structure will crash. Worse, the New England states will secede."

The secretary of the treasury also made it clear that if his plan for assuming the states' war debts was voted down again, he would resign.

Jefferson was stunned. "Perhaps," he said soothingly, "we should discuss this over dinner with Mr. Madison."

Hamilton agreed. When the three got together they made the following "deal":

• Hamilton would lobby his friends in New York, Philadelphia, and the northeast to vote for establishing the temporary location of the government in Philadelphia for ten years. During that period, the permanent location would be constructed near Georgetown on the Potomac River.

• In exchange, Madison and Jefferson would urge their friends in the South to support Hamilton's financial plan.

Since only a few votes were needed to clinch both proposals, the trade-off worked perfectly. By the middle of July, Washington had signed both bills.

Although he took no part in the debate or compromise, Washington was delighted by the outcome.

"The two great questions of funding the debt and fixing the seat of Government were always considered by me as questions of the most delicate nature," he wrote later. "They were more in danger of having convulsed the

Government itself than any other points. I hope they are now settled in as satisfactory a manner as could have been expected."

Not everyone was happy, however. "We may as well have a set of gamblers for rulers," cried the *Boston Gazette.*

Long before the bills were passed to establish the permanent seat of government and the methods of getting the nation out of debt, little Rhode Island had ratified the Constitution. The thirteen states were once again united, bringing a cry of joy from George Washington.

"Since the bond of union is now complete and we once more consider ourselves as one family, it is much to be hoped that reproaches will cease and prejudices be done away; for we should all remember that we are members of that community upon whose general success depends our particular and individual welfare," he said on receiving the news. "If we mean to support the liberty and independence which it has cost us so much blood and treasure to establish, we must drive far away the demon of party spirit and local reproach."

To help heal the wounds created by Rhode Island's long estrangement, Washington visited the tiny state as soon Congress adjourned in August 1790.

Washington spent most of his time in Newport and Providence and took in every point of interest the two cities had to offer. He also visited five private homes, staying long enough to chat with the owners and share a glass of wine or punch.

As always, various organizations honored him with presentations and speeches. Each time, he responded warmly and thoughtfully. To the Jewish Congregation of Newport, for example, he said: "It is now no more that toleration is spoken of, as it was by indulgence of one class of people, that another enjoyed the exercise of their inherent natural rights. For happily the Government of the United States, which gives bigotry no sanction, to persecution no assistance, requires only that they who live together under its protection should, as good citizens, [give] it on all occasions their effectual support."

To the members of the Rhode Island legislature, he pointed out it was up to "the people themselves to preserve and promote the great advantages of their political and natural situation."

Toward the end of August, Washington left New York, bound for the temporary capital in Philadelphia. After a brief visit, during which time he selected and moved into a new residence for the presidency, he went to Mount Vernon for a vacation.

When he returned to duty, he faced a new political storm; not in Congress this time, but in his own domain.

His painful experience during the Revolution as the commander in chief of a poorly equipped and often starving army taught Washington three key lessons:

• The nation could not survive with a weak central government.

• The nation could not prosper when thirteen state governments were issuing money and competing with each other financially.

• To progress, the states must pool their resources and deal with the outside world as a single, unified power.

As a result, he was delighted with the early results produced by Hamilton's financial plans.

"Our revenues have been considerably more productive than it was imagined they would be," he crowed in a letter to a friend in France. Washington also said crops were plentiful and bringing "great prices."

Before Congress adjourned in 1790, the House of Representatives had asked the secretary of the Treasury whether any further action should be taken to boost "the public credit" of the United States.

Quick to respond, Hamilton urged Congress to take two additional, but critical steps: first, to impose higher taxes on imported spirits and on liquor distilled in the United States; and second, to establish a "national" bank to be called "The Bank of the United States." (Only two banks were in existence at the time.)

Southerners were generally opposed to the higher internal taxes, since most of the whiskey was produced in Southern states and on the frontier. They also objected to the bank proposal, claiming that it was "unconstitutional" because the Constitution made no mention of a provision for such a bank. In addition, they feared the bank would give too much power to the financial centers in the North.

After a lengthy and heated debate, both measures passed. Before becoming law, however, they required Washington's signature.

Deeply concerned about the bank bill, the president hesitated. Was it "unconstitutional" as many of its opponents claimed? He asked his Secretaries for their opinions.

Jefferson said Congress did not have the authority to create the bank. Edmund Randolph, the attorney general, agreed.

Washington passed these opinions on to Hamilton and asked for his response, "so that I may be fully possessed of the argument for and against the measure before I express any opinion of my own."

As he waited for Hamilton to reply, Washington asked his old friend, Madison, to prepare a veto message for him should he refuse to sign the bank bill.

If Washington was going to veto the bank measure, Madison suggested he use these key words: "I object to the bill because it is an essential principle of Government that powers not delegated by the Constitution cannot rightfully be exercised; because the power proposed by the bill to be exercised is not delegated; and because I cannot satisfy myself that it results from an expressed power by fair and safe rules of implication."

In a 15,000-word defense of his proposal, this was Hamilton's basic position: "Every power vested in a government is in its nature sovereign, and includes, by force of the term, a right to employ all the means requisite and fairly applicable to the attainment of the ends of such power." In other words, the Constitution contained "implied powers" that the government had a right to use.

No! said Jefferson and Madison; the government did not have such powers and must stick to the letter of the law.

Now, Washington had to decide. He could either sign the bill, refuse to sign it, and, by doing so, allow it to become law, or, for the first time, exercise his power of veto.

He signed the bank bill on February 25, 1791. Six days later, he signed the tax measure. When he did so, he unwittingly ignited a war of words and ideas that pitted Madison and Jefferson against Hamilton forever.

During the spring and summer of 1790, a war broke out on the frontier between settlers and several tribes of Indians.

Many of the Indian tribes were in the northwest and, Washington believed, were being encouraged by the British, who traded with them constantly and supplied them with arms, to retain a foothold in the area. These Indians, including the Cherokees, Shawnees, and Miamis, were murdering white settlers and burning their homes as they moved westward. Other tribes, mainly Chickasaws, Choctaws, and Creeks, were in the Southwest, where they were backed by the Spanish.

Washington believed every effort should be made to maintain peace with the Indians. "We must work out formal treaties with them that recognize their territorial rights," he told Jefferson. "And we must treat them with fairness and justice. If any of the tribes want war, however, we should give them war."

For a time, it appeared that Washington had defused hostilities when he invited a twenty-nine-man delegation of Creek Indians to New York to sign a treaty related to a dispute that had arisen over land claims in Georgia.

After the treaty was signed, Washington entertained the Indians in his home, gave them a formal military review, and arranged for a visit aboard the *America*, a ship that had just completed a voyage to China.

Washington signed the treaty in the Hall of Congress in New York and after doing so, shook the hand of each Indian.

The situation in the Northwest became so volatile, however, that Washington ordered troops under Major General Arthur St. Clair to advance from Fort Washington (now Cincinnati, Ohio) some 135 miles in a northwesterly direction and establish a strong military post at Miami Village.

Before the army left on its mission, Washington told St. Clair, "As an old soldier, and as one whose early life was particularly engaged in Indian warfare, I feel competent to counsel in three words: beware of surprise. Again and again, General, beware of surprise."

In supplementing these orders, Secretary of War Henry Knox told General St. Clair that once the post was established, he was to "seek the enemy" and "strike them with severity." A year later, when these orders were carried out, they would prove to be the biggest military mistake that the Washington administration ever made.

❧ "I now have the painful task to give you an account of as unfortunate an action as almost any that has been fought, in which every corps was engaged and worsted."

This was the gist of a message Washington received in Philadelphia from General St. Clair on December 9, 1791, just as one of Martha's Friday-evening receptions was getting under way.

By Monday, Washington was able to piece together what had happened: The troops had been encamped along a creek feeding the Wabash River near the Ohio-Indiana line (now Mercer County, Ohio) early in November. At sunrise on December 3, a breakdown in communications enabled hundreds of Indians to surprise and surround some 1,500 of St. Clair's men. After a fierce three-hour battle, St. Clair's troops somehow managed to break out of the encirclement to the rear and escape.

In what would ultimately be the worst defeat U.S. soldiers ever suffered at the hands of Indians, the Americans lost more than nine hundred men, sixty-eight of them officers. Many more were wounded. In addition, they lost all of their artillery and most of their arms and supplies.

St. Clair's dispatch added grimly, "The most disgraceful part of the business is that the greatest part of the men threw away their arms and accoutrements, even after the pursuit had ceased."

Despite this setback, Washington kept up a strong effort to achieve peace on the frontier and made some progress. But in the Northwest, the British kept reminding the Indians that if they wished to keep their hunting grounds, they should ignore American peace offerings and continue their raids on western settlements. As further encouragement, the British continued to give the Indians arms, liquor, and gifts as they had done for years.

While he was not a man to boast, Washington had every right to be proud of the accomplishments of his first thirty-six months in office.

Among the landmark bills passed by Congress and signed into law by the president were the following:

- The census act, requiring a census to be taken every ten years
- The first patent act
- The first copyright act
- Authorization, given to Washington, for construction of a "federal city" as the permanent capital
- Funding plans, including that for the national bank
- Admission of Vermont and Kentucky as the fourteenth and fifteenth states
- Adoption of the Bill of Rights
- Creation of a permanent post office
- The Mint or Coinage Act

In addition, the nation's revenues had rapidly increased, its credit was safely established, its money was stabilized, and its supply of capital greatly expanded; in short, the nation was thriving.

For all this to have been achieved by an old, established government in such a short period of time would have been remarkable. For a brand-new government, beset by complicated problems resulting from relations with tribes of hostile Indians and foreign governments, it was a truly astonishing record.

Between the winter of 1791 and the spring of 1792, however, Washington faced another serious crisis. Again, it erupted in his Cabinet. And again, it stemmed from the feud between Hamilton and Jefferson.

In another of his famous reports, Alexander Hamilton suggested the government should encourage manufacturing "to render the United States independent of foreign nations." While he admitted that "cultivation of the earth" was more important than "every other kind of industry," its interests could be advanced by the "due encouragement of manufacture."

In his report, filed with the House of Representatives on December 5, 1791, Hamilton said he believed the United States should manufacture "all the necessary weapons of war" and not leave "these essential implements of national defense" to private enterprise.

To encourage industrial development, Hamilton suggested that the government subsidize industry, establish protective tariffs, give prizes to inventors, and improve roads and canals. He also insisted that the Constitution gave the government authority to support such programs.

"There seems to be no room for a doubt that whatever concerns the general interests of learning, of agriculture, of manufactures, and of commerce are within the sphere of the national councils," he said.

Hamilton's proposals brought a howl of protest from Jefferson and his friends who believed that Hamilton wanted to convert the new "republic" into a monarchy.

Jefferson argued that Hamilton's interpretation of the Constitution made it "a very different thing from what the people thought they had submitted to."

Madison agreed. "If Congress accepts Hamilton's proposals, the Constitution had better be thrown into the fire at once," he pointed out angrily.

This fierce argument among three of the smartest and most powerful men in the nation escalated into personal attacks printed in newspapers under pen names such as "Catullus," "Metullus," "Aristides," "Sidney," and "Farmer."

Washington, pained by the feud, tried to bring it to an end. He wrote to Jefferson and Hamilton and asked for "mutual forbearance" to preserve the Union which, he said, "has the fairest prospect of happiness and prosperity that ever was presented to man."

When both replied, Washington realized there would be no truce. What he didn't foresee, however, was that Hamilton and Jefferson had laid the foundation for a political system dominated by two parties. And while these parties have had many labels since Washington's time, today they are known as the Democrats and Republicans.

 By the time Congress was ready to adjourn for a vacation in May 1792, Washington had decided he would retire.

"It's time to go home for good," he told Martha one evening as they readied for bed.

"I agree," she said softly.

Within a few days, in separate meetings, he made his decision known to his Cabinet members—Jefferson, Knox, Hamilton, and Randolph. All tried to dissuade him. He thanked them for their kind words and thoughts, but stuck to his decision. Now, he must decide how and when to announce his plans. He asked James Madison for his advice.

Madison, like the others, tried to convince Washington that he should stand for a second term.

"This is a critical time," Madison said. "The country needs you now as much as before."

"I am sixty years old," Washington said. "My health is declining. And it is aggravated by the attacks on our policies and the growing discontent among members of Congress and especially in my own department."

"But there have been no attacks against you," Hamilton pointed out. "And you have not been the source of the discontent."

Madison insisted that if Washington stayed at the helm another four years, the government's enemies would fade away.

"If you retire, who would become president?" Madison asked. "Jefferson? He won't accept if nominated. Adams? Since he favors a monarchy he can't get elected. And neither can John Jay for the same reason."

Washington didn't respond, except to say that he had not changed his mind. He asked Madison to prepare a farewell speech for him that would be given at some future date.

As the days passed, it became clearer to Washington that the public and his advisers wished him to agree to a second term. He remained silent, however. And that silence was taken as consent.

On February 13, 1793, Washington was re-elected as president. And, for the second time, unanimously.

Long before Washington's re-election, a revolution had erupted in France. Early in 1793, King Louis XVI was beheaded, 20,000 alleged enemies of the French Revolution were executed, and France had declared war on Great Britain, Holland, and Spain.

Washington now faced a delicate problem: Should the United States recognize the new French regime?

During a hot debate in a Cabinet meeting, Jefferson favored recognition. He pointed out that thousands of Americans, mindful of their own revolution against a monarchy, were supportive of the French revolutionaries.

"If we don't recognize this government, the French and our own people will be furious," Jefferson said. "And why wouldn't they be? Without France's financial and military support we certainly could not have won our own revolution."

Hamilton admitted that the colonies could not have thrown off the yoke of British rule without French aid. Still, he was opposed to recognizing the newly established French government. He noted that every other government in Europe was a monarchy.

"If the United States were to recognize France, it would appear that we were encouraging more revolutions," he said. "Our country is only four years old. We have no navy and virtually no army. We are just getting on our feet financially. Why invite the enmity of countries we are trying to engage in trade? Why take sides?"

After listening to all the arguments, Washington made up his mind. He signed a statement that read: "We surely cannot deny to any nation that right whereon our own government is founded, that every nation may govern itself according to whatever form it pleases."

Unhappily, this brave, statesmanlike pronouncement widened the breach between Hamilton and Jefferson and their respective followers. And while it pleased France, it irritated England and every monarchy in Europe.

As the time for Washington's second inaugural approached, it became clear that the French Revolution had divided public opinion just as it had the association between Jefferson and Hamilton.

Sensing the unrest, Washington asked his Cabinet whether the swearing-in should be public or private and with or without ceremony.

For a change, Hamilton and Jefferson were in agreement. With pro-French and pro-British mobs roaming the streets, they urged Washington to take the oath in the president's house with only Cabinet members present. Knox and Randolph protested.

"We should have a parade!" Knox insisted. "We ought to impress people with the importance of the office of the president of the United States."

Washington chose a middle course. On March 4, 1793, he appeared in the Senate chamber without escort and gave a two-paragraph inaugural speech, the shortest in American history. When it was over, he was sworn in, left the chamber, got into his carriage alone, and rode home. The entire affair probably took no more than two hours.

Later, newspapers quoted Washington as saying he was now embarked on four more years of "slavery."

After the inaugural, Congress adjourned and the Washingtons went home to Mount Vernon, arriving there April 2. Less than a week later, they hurried back to Philadelphia, convinced the country faced serious trouble.

Edmond Charles Genet, a minister representing the new French government, had arrived in Charleston, Washington learned, and was recruiting American privateers.

"This means American vessels and crews will soon be raiding British cargo ships and sharing whatever valuables they find aboard," he told Martha.

Clearly, such piracy could involve the United States in a war with England; a country that still had military posts on American soil and a navy powerful enough to blockade every American port.

Since it would take almost two months to pull Congress together, Washington realized he would somehow have to act alone if there was any hope of keeping the nation neutral. But could he do so without violating the Constitution, which said that the president must check with Congress before making any major change in foreign policy?

Before he rushed northward, Washington summoned his Cabinet to a meeting on April 19 in Philadelphia to determine how the United States could avoid being drawn into a war with either France or England. By the time the president got to Philadelphia, Chief Justice John Jay had prepared a position paper for the Cabinet to consider.

Despite a heated and lengthy debate, the president and his Cabinet reached a unanimous decision: The president would not recall Congress, but issue a "proclamation" saying the United States would "pursue a conduct friendly and impartial" toward the belligerent powers, meaning France and England. The proclamation, signed by Washington on April 22, also called on all citizens to "carefully avoid all acts and proceedings whatsoever, which in any manner tend to contravene such disposition."

Those who became involved in the war between France and England, the proclamation warned, would "receive no protection from the United States, and those who engaged in belligerency within the jurisdiction of American courts would be prosecuted."

To avoid the appearance of deciding foreign policy without the approval of Congress, the word "neutrality" was not used. But the intent of the proclamation was quite clear: The United States was determined to remain at peace with all nations.

Washington's move came too late. The very day he signed the proclamation, a French war vessel captured a British ship named *Grange* in Delaware Bay and sailed it into Philadelphia.

Convinced that he had the support of the American people, "Citizen" Genet, as he called himself, continued to put American arms and crews aboard American ships and rush them to sea. Genet even awarded American pirate crews two captured British brigantines and began shipping ammunition to France.

"Citizen" Edmond Genet and his antagonistic ways caused President Washington much trouble.

"He's acting as judge and jury in a court proceeding on our soil," Washington fumed in a Cabinet meeting.

Genet was encouraged in his actions by a strong wave of American enthusiasm and support for the French Revolution. When he first heard of the president's proclamation, Genet hurried to Philadelphia, certain he could persuade Washington to change his position. He failed.

Unfazed, Genet began arming *Little Sarah,* a captured English ship—in Philadelphia—right under Washington's nose!

Jefferson warned Genet that sending *Little Sarah* to sea would be "a very serious offense." But Genet was defiant.

"Let me beseech you not to permit any attempt to put men on board her," Genet said. "She is filled with high-spirited patriots, and they will unquestionably resist." Genet also said that if the United States tried to detain *Little Sarah,* he would "appeal to the people."

When Washington received this report from Jefferson, he was furious. "He's threatening to do battle with us in our own waters!" he cried. "And he's threatening the office of the president!"

Despite official protests, Genet sent *Little Sarah* into the Atlantic. In the following months he also:

• said publicly that Washington's opinions were contrary to the wishes of his people.

• declared that he had recruited 1,500 seamen and would put them aboard American ships in American ports.

• continued to criticize Washington and called on Americans to prepare for war against England.

• recruited troops in several southern states to attack Spanish possessions in Florida and at the mouth of the Mississippi River.

Helpless to do anything else, Washington laid the facts before the French government in an eight-thousand-word report and asked that Genet be recalled.

The French promptly replaced Genet with Jean Antoine Joseph Baron Fauchet. When Fauchet arrived, he wanted to arrest Genet and return him to France. Fearing Genet would face the guillotine, Washington said, "No!" and gave the Frenchman political asylum.

During the summer of 1793 the government's attention suddenly switched from national and international politics to a serious domestic matter: health.

Early in August, several people in Philadelphia fell ill, turned yellow, and died. Within two weeks, "yellow fever" had reached epidemic proportions, killing scores every day.

At the time, it was not known that the infection was carried by mosquitoes. It was believed that people caught the fever from each other. As a result, thousands fled the city. Those who remained stayed off the streets as much as possible. When they did venture forth, they masked their mouths and noses. If someone approached, they would hurry to the other side of the street.

Although Congress had adjourned, Washington remained at his post. Toward the end of August, he told Martha, "You and the children had better start for Mount Vernon."

"Fine," she said. "But you're going with us." Washington knew that tone of voice all too well. A few days later, the whole family left the city. It was probably a fortunate move. By the time the epidemic died down, four thousand were dead.

 "Woods, swamps and naked hills . . ."

That was the way a lawyer named James Kent described the ten square miles of real estate ceded to the national government by Maryland and Virginia on the banks of the Potomac River; a tract of land that was to become the nation's capital.

Kent said the broad avenues planned by Major Pierre Charles L'Enfant, a French designer hired by Washington, "were all cut through woods" with "here and there a house and hut." While Kent was enthusiastic about the financial prospects for the city, he was also charmed by the dramatic views from the hilltops.

He noted that the president's house, on a site Washington had selected, was "a mile from the river on a hill yielding a gentle declivity to the river and commanding a fine view for several miles down the river."

The building was to be made of "grayish-white free stone handsomely polished," he added and "presages to be the grandest and most elegant palace in the whole world."

President Washington arrived at the site early on September 10, 1793. Excited and delighted, he joined fellow Masons and a score of dignitaries in an elaborate parade to the Capitol for a ceremony marking the laying of the cornerstone.

The parade began promptly at 10 A.M. It was not a very orderly parade, as the participants often had to pass single file around stumps and holes along a narrow trail through the woods. And when they came to Tiber Creek, they found the water so high that they had to cross on a single slippery log.

On reaching the southeast corner of the Capitol, the group formed a circle facing west. A moment of silence was shattered by a round of artillery fire.

As the echoes died away, Washington placed a plaque on the cornerstone with a prayer. Joseph Clark, a Masonic dignitary, then made a long speech punctuated by eleven more volleys.

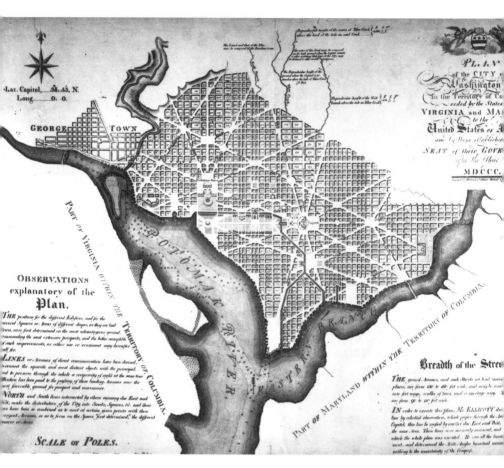

The plan for the permanent capital of the United States, rendered by Major Pierre Charles L'Enfant, was considered a work of art, although it was disliked by Thomas Jefferson.

It was, one newspaper reported, "the grandest exhibit ever."

While many—including Secretary of State Thomas Jefferson—did not like L'Enfant's grandiose plans for the capital, the plans received

Washington's whole-hearted support and ultimately yielded what was considered a great work of art.

But the project did not go smoothly. In fact, L'Enfant, carried away with his own importance, created so many problems he was fired before the project was completed.

There were also all kinds of delays related to financing and construction. The government did not move into its new quarters until 1800.

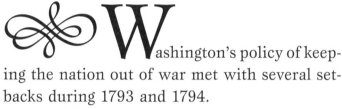ashington's policy of keeping the nation out of war met with several setbacks during 1793 and 1794.

Trouble first erupted on the northwestern frontier, when Lord Dorchester, Governor-General of Canada, set up a supply base deep in American territory, killing all attempts by President Washington to establish peace with the Indians.

Washington felt that the British were mostly responsible for the murders of helpless women and children along the frontier. "I suspect their soldiers, dressed and painted as Indians, are participating in the raids," he fumed.

In a letter to John Jay, he asked, "Can it be expected, I ask, so long as these things are encouraged, that there will ever be any cordiality between our two countries? No!" Unless the British would give up their western posts in U.S. territory, Washington said, war with England "will be inevitable."

Washington promptly ordered General Anthony Wayne to the Miami River with three thousand men. This brought an immediate reaction from the British, who believed Wayne was about to attack Canada.

"Lord Dorchester has now promised his Indian friends that we will soon be at war with England," Washington told his Cabinet at a hastily called meeting early in 1793. "And he told the Indians that they and the British will share the Northwest Territory once we are defeated."

Hamilton was shocked.

"And who is the source of this information?" he asked.

"In confidence, Governor Clinton."

A source friendly to the United States had passed the information on to the New York governor, Washington said.

"It is clear that Lord Dorchester hopes to lower the northern boundary between this nation and Canada," Washington went on. "Obviously, if such an attempt is made, we must retaliate," he concluded.

Washington said he asked Clinton to forward all the intelligence he could gather, especially about the strength of British troops along the border.

Relations worsened rapidly when the British navy began attacking American ships in the Atlantic, confiscating cargo, and forcing captured American seamen to serve aboard British vessels.

Dashing hopes for improved French-American relations after the Genet incident, the French soon issued similar orders: American ships carrying goods to and from England were to be captured and all cargo seized!

Both the administration and Congress were thrown into a tizzy by these developments. All manner of suggestions were made: Raise an army of 20,000 men! Halt all trade with England and France! Fortify every port! Raise a navy to protect American ships!

Short of a declaration of war, no effective way was found to cope with this alarming and complicated situation. Finally, in the spring of 1794, soon after Secretary of State Thomas Jefferson retired to his Virginia plantation, Washington appointed Chief Justice John Jay as a special envoy to England and James Monroe as ambassador to France. Keep the United States out of war, they were told, but try to settle all outstanding problems and disputes.

In mid-June 1794, only two months after the two envoys left American shores, another crisis confronted Washington; this one created by his own people.

The excise tax on whiskey, passed as part of Hamilton's plan to keep the nation from going bankrupt, was denounced as unfair by many farmers in western Pennsylvania for two principal reasons.

First, the economy of the frontier depended on barter. One merchant, for example, advertised that he would accept "Cash, flour, whiskey, beef, pork, bacon, wheat, rye, oats, corn, ashes, candlewick, tallow, furs, snakeroot, furs, etc." for his wares. Cash, however, was virtually nonexistent.

When crops were not damaged by early fall frosts or early spring floods, the poverty-stricken farmers reaped good harvests of grain. But large quantities of grain could not be shipped east over the mountains. Nor could it be moved to major population centers by water since the Mississippi was blocked by Spain.

Converted into whiskey, however, some grain could be shipped and the rest used for barter, the mainstay of the poor western farm communities. In one Pennsylvania county alone, there were five hundred stills. Because of taxes, frontier owners everywhere faced this difficult question: How could they pay a tax without cash?

Second, as the frontier farmers saw it, the government failed to open the Mississippi to navigation and could not protect them from the Indians. Why, then, should they pay a federal tax? "To be subject to all the burdens and enjoy none of the benefits arising from government is what we will never submit to," one group of rebels said.

According to federal law, the excise tax was to be collected at the point where the whiskey was made. Many farmers, however, banded together and refused to pay the tax. Often, the dissidents burned the stills of those who were willing to pay, and threatened their lives.

And when federal agents showed up, some were tarred and feathered and chased out of the mountains. In a typical case, excise collector Robert Johnson was assaulted by sixteen men disguised as women. The "women" cut off Johnson's hair, covered him with tar and feathers, stole his horse, and left him stranded in the forest.

Later, the home of John Neville, an excise inspector, was attacked. When authorities came to Neville's rescue, a man was killed and Neville's house was burned to the ground.

In early August 1794, some seven thousand rebellious farmers gathered together to air their grievances. The same day, a horseman rode through Pittsburgh, a community of only four hundred inhabitants, and threatened to burn it. As he rode along the main street, he waved a tomahawk and shouted, "It is not only the excise law that must go down; your district and associate judges must go down; your high offices and salaries."

When word of all this reached Philadelphia late in the summer of 1794, Edmund Randolph told a Cabinet meeting, "There is a civil war going on in Washington County. And it may very well spread to the western frontiers of other states."

Washington was truly alarmed. Kentucky was already threatening secession. If that idea caught on, it could bring the nation to its knees.

"Congress has addressed the grievances of these people many times," he said angrily. "But they continue to defy the law. If we allow it to continue, we will be faced with nothing but anarchy and confusion."

It was agreed that Governor Mifflin should immediately call out the Pennsylvania militia to bring order to the region. Mifflin refused.

Since the tiny American army in existence at the time was with Anthony Wayne in the Northwest, Hamilton said the federal government had no choice but to put down the farmers' rebellion.

"We should call out the militia of the four nearby states and march into Washington County to enforce the law," Hamilton said.

Would the states comply? the Cabinet wondered. Would the militia of one state cross the boundary of another?

Washington, having faced and put down mutinies during the Revolution, said, "I am willing to take the risk. First, however, we should try to find a peaceable solution." The Cabinet agreed.

With an appeal to "reason, virtue and patriotism," Washington sent three commissioners to the western frontier to settle matters with the rebellious whiskey makers. "Offer amnesty to all if they will stop trying to obstruct the law," Washington told the commissioners as they left his office in Philadelphia.

The commissioners soon scurried back from their mission. The frontier was in utter chaos, they said.

"The rebels are declaring independence from the United States and terrorizing those who were willing to pay the excise tax," one commissioner reported.

"And they say they'll kill any federal agents who show up in their territory," another chimed in.

"How strong is their group?" Washington wanted to know.

"At least seven thousand," was the response.

On September 25, having assessed all intelligence from the West, Washington called out some 12,000 members of four state militias. When they came together at the designated staging area in Bedford, Pennsylvania, they would form an army as large as any Washington had had during the Revolution.

On September 30th, dressed in his old uniform, the sixty-two-year-old president left the Capital, once again ready to join American troops in battle.

At Washington's side as he rode away from the president's house at midmorning of the 30th was Alexander Hamilton, who would act for Secretary of War Henry Knox, then in New England.

The first overnight stop was to be at a place called Trap (now Trappe), some twenty-five miles northwest of Philadelphia. As Washington and his small group approached the town, he was overtaken by a rider on a hot horse; a Major Stagg, who was the head clerk in the Department of War.

With the outbreak of the Whiskey Rebellion, Washington again donned his military uniform.

"Important message from General Wayne, sir," Stagg said, drawing a letter and other documents from his saddlebag. Washington's face lit up as he read the lines.

"Great news!" he exulted to Hamilton and his other companions. "Wayne has destroyed all the Indian settlements along the Miami River, an area of some five thousand acres. He also confiscated the stores of the British agent of Indian affairs who was foolish enough to establish a supply base away from his garrison."

In what was known as the "Battle of Fallen Timbers," Wayne's force of nine hundred well-drilled men soundly defeated more than two thousand Indians who had been encouraged and supplied by the British.

The victory would ultimately have a profound impact on relations with Great Britain and assure the loyalty of western frontiersmen.

By prearrangement, Washington met members of the New Jersey and Pennsylvania militias at a camp established near Carlisle, Pennsylvania, early in October.

On his arrival, he quickly set to work organizing the troops for the march westward to a rendezvous at Bedford with units from Maryland and Virginia.

On the 9th, he met with William Findley and William Redick, members of a "Committee of Safety" representing the four western counties at the heart of the rebellion. At first, the two expressed concern about a confrontation between the whiskey rebels and the troops.

"Many of our people think that the rest of the country is just as resentful of the excise taxes as they," William Findley said. "And most believe that the army would never march against them. While these people seem ready to obey the law, I think it will be necessary afterward to protect the offices where the taxes are to be collected."

Washington assured the two men that the government did not intend to "coerce" the local population. He made it clear, however, that the march would continue to convince the rebels that the government "would and could enforce obedience to the laws."

By the time Washington crossed the Blue Ridge Mountains and arrived at Bedford, it was clear the rebels had received his message. There would be no opposition to the army. The Whiskey Rebellion was over.

Washington promptly announced that he would return to Philadelphia to be on hand for the opening of Congress on November 3. Before he left, he addressed the troops with these words: "No citizens of the United States can ever be engaged in a service more important to the country. It is nothing less than to consolidate and to preserve the blessings of that Revolution which, at the expense of blood and treasure, made us a free and independent nation."

He closed by saying that the army had two objectives: First, to subdue all who were in armed opposition to the "national will and authority," and second, to help local authorities "bring offenders to justice."

When the army reached the frontier, several suspected of involvement in the rebellion were rounded up and prosecuted. Only two, however, were indicted for treason.

On a bleak day in March 1795, Washington waved a thick document at Edmund Randolph, his new secretary of state, and said darkly, "This must be kept secret from every person on Earth until it is delivered under seal to the Senate!"

The document was the treaty John Jay had signed with Great Britain. Because of delays at sea, however, a copy didn't reach Washington until almost five months later. By then, Congress had adjourned.

"The terms of this treaty are going to divide and arouse the passions of our people," Washington said. "Some terms are clearly pro-French and others pro-British."

"I agree," Randolph said, "But whatever you do, will the Senate go along?"

Washington had no illusions about the decision he faced. If he refused to ratify, the French and their supporters would be delighted, since it could mean war with England and the United States having to turn to France for help. If he did ratify, it could bring about serious internal disturbances and eventual war with France.

Washington carefully weighed these facts: The United States was only six years old. It had no navy and virtually no army. It was just beginning to get out of debt and starting to prosper. It was surrounded by powerful potential enemies: Britain in the North and Northwest, Spain in the Southeast and Southwest.

"The main objective of Jay's mission has been accomplished," he said firmly. "I will ratify with the proviso that Article XII be renegotiated."

Almost three months later, on June 8, Congress met in a special session after a long recess. As soon as the doors were closed in the Senate chamber, Vice President Adams gaveled for silence and read the following terse message from the president: "Gentlemen of the Senate: In pursuance of my nomination of John Jay, as Envoy Extraordinary to his Britannic Majesty on the 16th of April, 1794, and of the advice and consent of the Senate thereto on the 19th, a negotiation was opened in London. On the 7th of March, 1795, the treaty resulting there from was delivered to the Secretary of State. I now transmit to the Senate that treaty, and other documents connected with it. They will therefore in their wisdom decide whether they will advise and consent that the said treaty be made between the United States and his Britannic Majesty."

The treaty included twenty-eight articles. Many were still in dispute but would be worked out by commissioners representing each side. Americans would find many others hard to accept, however.

Article XII, for example, stipulated that while American ships could trade with the West Indies, these ships would be limited in size to seventy tons. And under this article, U.S. vessels could not carry West Indies products—sugar, cotton, and molasses—to other nations; in particular, France. Equally irritating was the fact that the treaty was silent on the British practice of capturing American seamen and forcing them to work on British ships.

There was, however, a major concession: The British agreed to evacuate their military posts in the Northwest by the end of 1796. That would end British encouragement of Indian attacks on the western frontier.

Meeting in secret, the Senate hotly debated the terms of the Jay Treaty for three long weeks. Finally, by a vote of twenty to ten, it gave its "consent."

When John Jay returned to the United States in May 1795, he resigned as chief justice and became governor of New York.

The treaty he helped fashion, however, drew fierce attacks from both pro-French and pro-English supporters. One mob of French sympathizers, for example, hanged Jay in effigy. Another stoned Alexander Hamilton and drove him from a platform on a New York city street when he tried to explain the terms of the Jay Treaty.

In Philadelphia, a mob threatened the home of the French minister. Similar incidents took place in other cities.

And Washington—for the first time in his political career—was openly attacked for ratifying the treaty.

While the Jay Treaty did not satisfy everyone, it paid an unexpected and handsome dividend: Spain, in what became known as the Treaty of San Lorenzo, evacuated her posts north of the southern boundary of the United States and opened the Mississippi to navigation.

"At last," Washington told his Cabinet when he heard the news, "the United States now has full control of her territory. And we remain at peace."

Suddenly, however, the House of Representatives threatened to nullify the Jay Treaty!

The House voted sixty-two to thirty-seven that it had the right to reconsider treaties even though they had already become law.

In mid-March 1796, a month after the Jay Treaty went into effect, House leaders Albert Gallatin and Edward Livingston demanded that Washington give the House every document pertaining to the treaty for review. The House was saying, in effect, that if it didn't like what it found, it had the power to void the treaty.

Washington was furious. "The Constitution is clear!" he told his Cabinet as it wrestled with the problem. "The House can have no voice in treaty-making. The members who insist they do are trying to sabotage the Jay Treaty. And if they are successful, where will it lead us?"

All in the meeting knew the answer: The British would not give up their military posts in the West, again setting the frontier aflame. And all the other advantages Jay had negotiated—including the assurance of peace with England—would be lost.

"Worst of all," Washington pointed out, "the world will know that treaties signed with the United States would be meaningless."

Washington refused to give up the papers. After a stormy debate, the House backed down. The crisis was averted. The House never again interfered in treaty-making.

"To the PEOPLE of the United States

Friends and fellow citizens . . . "

Without explanation or embellishment, these words appeared on page two of a four-page Philadelphia newspaper, the *American Daily Advertiser* on September 19, 1796.

It was the headline for what later became known as Washington's "Farewell Address." Washington had begun working on the address a year earlier after writing to a nephew that he would "close my public life on March 4, 1797, after which no consideration under heaven" would lure him from "the walks of private life."

Washington began by saying that he had decided to "decline being considered" for reelection. (Electors would soon cast ballots in the third national election.)

"In withdrawing the tender of service which silence in my situation might imply," he said, "I am influenced by no diminution of zeal for your future interest, no deficiency of grateful respect for past kindness; but am supported by a full conviction that the step is compatible with both."

He acknowledged a "debt of gratitude" which he owed his "beloved country" for the honors it had bestowed on him and "still more for the steadfast confidence" with which it had supported him.

He hoped, he said, that "union and brotherly affection" among Americans would become "perpetual," and that the Constitution "may be sacredly maintained" and its administration "stamped with wisdom and virtue."

"The Unity of Government which constitutes you one people, is also now dear to you," he added. "It is justly so. For it is a main pillar in the edifice of your real independence, the support of your tranquility at home, your peace abroad, and of your safety, of your prosperity, of that very Liberty which you so highly prize."

He warned the nation against disunity or any attempt to "enfeeble the sacred ties" which linked "the various parts."

This portrait of President Washington was painted during his second term of office.

"The name of 'American' which belongs to you, in your national capacity, must always exalt the just pride of Patriotism, more than any appellation derived from local discriminations," he said. "With slight shades of difference, you have the same Religion, Manners, Habits, and political principles. You have in a common cause fought and triumphed together. The Independence and Liberty you possess are the work of joint councils, and joining efforts—of common dangers, sufferings and successes."

He then pointed out that the North, South, East, and West had much to give each other and if they remained united, Americans would enjoy greater strength and prosperity and "greater security from external danger."

Washington noted that the government was "the offspring of our own choice, uninfluenced and unawed, adopted upon full investigation and mature deliberation, completely free in its principles and in the distribution of its powers."

He urged Americans to respect authority, comply with the nation's laws, and guard their rights.

"The basis of our political systems is the right of the people to make and to alter their constitutions of Government," he continued. "But the Constitution which at any time exists is sacredly obligatory upon all."

"All obstructions to the execution of the laws; all combinations and association, with the real design to direct, control, counteract, or awe the regular deliberation of constituted authorities, are destructive of this fundamental principle, and of fatal tendency," he said.

Washington's address also included these important points:

• Citizens should be wary of various pressure groups that would try to undermine Constitutional authority.

• Politicians often misrepresent the opinions of other districts in order to strengthen influence in their own.

• Party politics hamper the president's efforts to act in the national interest.

• Americans should cultivate peace and harmony with all nations. In this regard, he said, "the nation which indulges toward another a habitual hatred or an habitual fondness is in some degree a slave."

• Europe had primary interests that did not relate to the United States. As a result, he urged that the nation "steer clear of permanent alliances, with any portion of the foreign world taking care always to keep ourselves, by suitable establishments, on a respectable defensive posture, we may safely trust to temporary alliances for extraordinary emergencies."

In conclusion, Washington said, he anticipated "with pleasing expectation" his retirement "in the midst of my fellow-citizens, the benign influence of good laws under a free government—the ever favorite object of my heart."

The presidential document was signed simply: "G. Washington."

Three months after releasing his Farewell Address, Washington went before Congress to deliver his eighth and final annual message.

Even though his term would not end until March 1797, his speech marked his last public appearance. It was not a long address, but it contained several important recommendations.

Washington called for the establishment of a strong navy, for example, saying, "It is our experience that the most sincere neutrality is not a sufficient guard against the deprivations of nations at war. To secure respect to a neutral flag, requires a naval force, organized and ready to vindicate it from insult and aggression." He asked for the creation of a military academy, a national university, and federal support for agriculture and manufacturing.

Washington also took the occasion to point out that the conditions of the Jay Treaty with

England were being carried out as agreed to. He did lament, however, that relations with France had deteriorated.

"Our trade has suffered," he said, "and is suffering extensive injuries from the cruisers and agents of the French republic."

Washington hoped, however, for harmony with France "consistent with a just and indispensable regard to the rights and honor of our country."

In conclusion, he said, "The situation in which I now stand, for the last time in the midst of the representatives of the people of the United States, recalls the period when the administration of the present form of government was commenced; and I cannot omit to congratulate you and my country on the success of the experiment."

Not long afterward, John Adams was elected the nation's second president and Thomas Jefferson vice president.

On March 3, as his last official act, Washington pardoned the men convicted of high treason in the Whiskey Rebellion. After attending Adams's inaugural the next day, he left Philadelphia for Mount Vernon.

Sixteen months later, President Adams believed the nation would soon be at war with France. For the second time, Washington was appointed head of the American Army. Now, however, his title was "Lieutenant General and Commander in Chief."

In an attempt to avoid a complete break in relations with France, President Adams sent a trio of commissioners across the Atlantic with instructions to try to settle grievances between the two countries.

The French refused to receive the ministers. They were told, however, that relations could be restored if the Americans would agree to several conditions, including these:

• Announce a change in policy toward France.

• Pay a bribe of $250,000 to the minister of foreign affairs.

• Offer the French government a $10 million loan to compensate for "insults" to France included in President Adams's inaugural speech.

When Congress learned about the behavior of the French early in 1798, it promptly ordered that an army of 10,000 men be raised immediately with plans made for another 50,000.

It also hurried completion of three of six frigates—the U.S.S. *Constitution*, *Constellation*, and *United States*—that Washington had asked for and signed into law in 1794.

The public, also outraged by the news from France, approved the steps taken by Congress and adopted a slogan: "Millions for Defense, but not one cent for Tribute!"

Not all fully supported what they considered to be signs of belligerence on the part of the United States, however. When the *Constitution* got stuck as she was being launched in Boston, a newspaper supporting Jefferson's followers said gleefully, "Oh frigate *Constitution*! Stay on shore!"

On receiving the summons to take command of the army, Washington immediately began to organize his top command and make initial plans for his troops.

By early 1799, however, French internal problems and military defeats caused her threat to peace in America to melt away, and Washington was able to give up his post and resume his retirement.

"Morning cloudy. Wind to northeast and mercury at 33. A large circle around the moon last night. At about ten o'clock it began to snow, soon after to hail, and then to a settled cold rain. Mercury 28 at night."

These words appeared in Washington's diary under the date of December 12, 1799. Despite the storm, Washington rode out at ten o'clock that morning to inspect his farms. He returned at three.

When Tobias Lear, his secretary, brought Washington's mail he asked, "Did you get wet?"

"No," Washington replied nonchalantly. "My greatcoat kept me dry."

"But your neck is wet and you have snow in your hair!" Lear protested.

"It's nothing," Washington insisted.

The next day, Washington had a sore throat. It worsened by the hour. Still, despite being hoarse, Washington cheerfully read several newspaper stories aloud to Martha and Lear as they sat with him in his study.

At three the next morning, his labored breathing caused Martha to wake up in alarm.

"Are you all right?" she asked worriedly.

"I'm, uh, hav—having trouble breathing," he gasped.

"I'll send for help."

"No. If you get up, you—you'll catch a cold."

Against her better judgment, Martha waited until daylight to send for an overseer named Rawlins, who normally cared for sick slaves. When he arrived at Washington's bedside, Washington indicated that he wanted to be bled, then the standard treatment for a serious illness.

Obediently, Rawlins made an incision in Washington's arm and began to draw blood from his body. "More," Washington croaked.

"No!" Martha said. "That's enough!"

By three that afternoon, three doctors were in attendance. And by then, despite Martha's protestations, Washington had been bled four times.

Two hours later, barely able to speak, Washington asked Martha to bring two wills from his desk.

"No, no," she said fearfully.

"Ess," he said with a weary nod of his head.

When Martha returned with the pair of wills, Washington indicated that one was obsolete and was to be burned; the other she was to safeguard.

Washington became weaker and weaker. Sometime that night, his words coming in gasps, he told Lear to see that he had a decent burial. And then, because he had a fear of being buried alive as many others did in his day, he asked Lear not to put his body in the family vault until three days had passed.

"Understand?"

"Yes," Lear murmured, tears rolling down his cheeks.

Shortly before midnight on December 14, Washington died. He was sixty-seven years old.

At a memorial service held at the request of Congress a short time later, his old comrade-in-arms, Congressman Henry "Light Horse Harry" Lee, eulogized the late president with these simple, but moving words:

"To the memory of the Man, first in war, first in peace, and first in the hearts of his countrymen."

Epilogue

Four days after Washington's death, a small group of friends and relatives left a grieving, distraught Martha at the manor house at Mount Vernon and accompanied her husband's body to the family tomb a short distance away. Leading the procession was a unit of the local militia. Behind, a groom led Washington's horse bearing an empty saddle, and a Masonic band, playing a somber dirge, followed as the mourners brought up the rear.

When the group reached the tomb, a schooner anchored in the Potomac fired several shots from cannons mounted on the deck. Eleven ar-

A small but reverent group accompanied George Washington's body to its final resting place in the family tomb on the grounds at Mount Vernon.

tillery pieces answered from the nearby shore. The Reverend Thomas Davis then read a short farewell over the lead-lined mahogany casket.

Within a few weeks, word of Washington's death had spread through the country and to Europe, touching off a wide range of tributes to the late president. One of the first was given by John Marshall, a staunch Washington supporter and a member of Congress.

"Our Washington is no more," Marshall wrote. "The Hero, the Sage and the Patriot of America—the man on whom in times of danger every eye was turned, and all hopes were placed—lives now only in his own great actions and in the hearts of an affectionate and afflicted people."

Before Martha died in 1802, members of Congress and others asked to have Washington's body moved from Mount Vernon to a crypt in the Capitol, which was not yet completed. Martha agreed on one condition: Her body would have to be interred next to her husband's.

While this condition was readily accepted, the effort to remove the remains of the Washingtons from Mount Vernon was repeatedly blocked by Southerners for a variety of reasons. The controversy came to an abrupt end in 1832, the centennial of Washington's birth, when family members said they would not allow the bodies to be moved from Mount Vernon.

In a tribute to Washington that same year, Senator Daniel Webster of Massachusetts, a great orator and lawyer, said, "Washington stands at the commencement of a new era, as well as at the head of the New World. A century from the birth of Washington changed the world. The country of Washington has been the theater on which a great part of the change has been wrought; and Washington himself a principal agent by which it has been accomplished. His age and his country are equally full of wonders; and of both he is the chief."

Ten years later, Abraham Lincoln said, "To add brightness to the sun or glory to the name of Washington is alike impossible. Let none attempt it. In silent awe pronounce the name, and in its naked deathless splendor leave it shining on."

In 1964, famed historian Samuel Eliot Morison wrote, "Washington's services in time of peace have never been adequately appreciated. His unique place in history rests not only on his superb leadership in war, and on his wise administration of the federal government; but even more on his integrity, good judgment, and magnanimity."

Despite his many accomplishments, one aspect of Washington's life and times troubled him: slavery. While he realized that the economy of the South depended on slave labor, Washington increasingly saw slavery as evil. In his will he freed his slaves, becoming the first major figure in the South to do so.

George Washington's actions and words made a deep impression on the minds and hearts of his countrymen. No other figure in American history has been honored so often and in so many unique ways. Throughout the United States, for example, the name "Washington" identifies bridges, streams, lakes, buildings, monuments, towns, counties, parks, and numerous other entities. "Washington" is also the name of a state and the nation's capital.

In addition, Washington's picture and likeness can be found in countless places, including schools, courthouses, federal buildings, and parks. It also adorns millions of dollar bills and twenty-five-cent pieces.

Why this is so is summed up best by George Bancroft, a highly respected historian and author of *The History Of The United States,* who said of Washington: "But for him, the country could not have achieved independence; but for him it could not have formed a union; but for him, it could not have set the federal government in successful motion."

George Washington, in other words, was truly the legendary "father of his country."

Suggestions and Acknowledgments

$\mathcal{T}$here is a vast pool of information about George Washington in the archives of various historical societies and libraries. Much of it is based on Washington's letters, diaries, official acts, and the letters and documents of others who were in contact with him during his lifetime. For those interested in learning more about Washington's role in the framing of the Constitution and his performance as president, the following books, which were the primary sources for this volume—and gratefully acknowledged—are recommended: *George Washington Papers*, by Frank Donovan; *The Whiskey Rebellion*, by Thomas P. Slaughter; *Through a Fiery Trial*, by Bob Arnebeck; *Patri-*

arch, by Richard Norton Smith; *Miracle in Philadelphia*, by Catherine Drinker Bowen; *The Creation of Washington, D.C.*, by Kenneth R. Bowling; *The History of the United States*, by George Bancroft; *Alexander Hamilton: Portrait in Paradox*, by John C. Miller; *George Washington*, by Douglas Southall Freeman (six volumes); *George Washington*, by James Thomas Flexner (four volumes); *The President's House*, by William Seale; *The Founding Fathers—George Washington*, edited by Ralph K. Andrist; *George Washington*, by W. E. Woodward; *The Young Alexander Hamilton*, by James Thomas Flexner; and *Thomas Jefferson*, by David Muzzey.

Thanks also to the personnel at the Chester County, Pennsylvania, Historical Society and to the Paoli, Tredyffrin, and Chester County libraries, as well as to the Free Public Library of Philadelphia for their help as the project went forward. In addition, thanks to Sara Landis for her comments and guidance on reading the early drafts of the manuscript as it progressed.

Special thanks go to Laura Walsh, my editor at The Millbrook Press, who painstakingly and diligently reviewed every line and nuance of this material and, aside from making routine corrections in spelling and grammar, offered numerous helpful suggestions and insightful comments, all of which strengthened the book considerably.

Important Dates

1787

February 2   Shays's Rebellion put down by Massachusetts militia.

May 25   Constitutional Convention opens with George Washington unanimously elected president.

September 17   Constitution signed by the delegates of twelve states. Ratification process begins almost immediately.

1788

June 25   Virginia becomes the ninth state to ratify the Constitution, making the new government operative.

1789

January 7   Presidential electors are chosen in all states that have ratified the Constitution.

February 4	Washington unanimously elected president.
April 30	Washington inaugurated as the first president of the United States.
June 1	Washington signs the first bill passed by Congress: the proper procedure for administering oaths of office.
July 27	Department of Foreign Affairs established. Name later changed to Department of State.
August 7	Department of War created.
August 22	The president appears in person in the Senate to obtain "advice and consent" concerning a treaty with the Creek Indians.
September 2	Treasury Department created.
September 9	Twelve amendments to the Constitution recommended by the House. Later, ten were ratified by the states and became the Bill of Rights.
October 15	Washington leaves New York for tour of New England states.

1790

January 8	Washington submits first annual message to Congress.
March 1	The law providing for a census every ten years is signed by Washington. The 1790 census establishes the population of the U.S. as 3,929,214.

| *July 16* | Permanent location for the seat of government is established near Georgetown on the Potomac River. The president is authorized to plan a federal city. |
| *December 8* | Washington delivers his second annual message to Congress. |

1791

February 25	The bill chartering the Bank of the United States is signed by Washington.
March 3	Excise tax levied on distilled liquor.
December 12	The First Bank of the United States opens in Philadelphia.

1792

| *April 2* | Mint or Coinage Act passed. |
| *December 5* | Presidential electors cast ballots. |

1793

February 13	Washington elected unanimously for second term.
March 4	Washington's second inaugural.
April 22	Washington signs "Proclamation of Neutrality."
August 28	Yellow fever breaks out in Philadelphia.
September 18	Washington lays cornerstone at the Capitol.

1794

April 16 Chief Justice John Jay nominated to negotiate a treaty with Britain.

July 17 The Whiskey Rebellion erupts in western Pennsylvania.

September 30 General Anthony Wayne reports victory at the Battle of Fallen Timbers on August 20.

November 19 Whiskey Rebellion ends. Jay's Treaty signed in London.

1795

June 24 Jay's Treaty ratified by Senate twenty to ten.

August 14 Washington signs Jay's Treaty.

October 27 Treaty of San Lorenzo signed in Spain, providing free navigation of the Mississippi and establishing southern boundary of U.S. at 31st parallel.

1796

September 19 Washington's Farewell Address appears in the *American Daily Advertiser*.

1797

February 9 John Adams elected president.

March 3 In last official act as president, Washington pardons those convicted of high treason in the Whiskey Rebellion.

March 15   Washington returns to Mount Vernon.

1798

July 2   Facing threat of war with France, Washington appointed lieutenant general and commander in chief of the army.

1799

December 14   Washington dies at Mount Vernon.